FIFTH SUNDAY

Poetry Books by Rita Dove

The Yellow House on the Corner (Carnegie-Mellon
    University Press, 1980)
Museum (Carnegie-Mellon, 1983)
Thomas and Beulah (Carnegie-Mellon, 1986)

Limited Editions

Ten Poems (Penumbra Press, 1977)
The Only Dark Spot in the Sky (Porch Publications, 1980)
Mandolin (Ohio Review Poetry Series, 1982)

FIFTH SUNDAY

Stories by

RITA DOVE

Volume One
in the Callaloo Fiction Series
Published at the University of Kentucky
Lexington, 1985

First Edition, 1985

Acknowledgements are made to *The Southern Review* and *Gargoyle*, respectively, for the following stories which first appeared in their pages: "Second-Hand Man" and "The Spray Paint King."

Cover photo and design by Fred Viebahn

ISBN: 0-912759-06-2

The publication of this volume is supported in part by a grant from the Kentucky Arts Council with funds from the National Endowment for the Arts.

CALLALOO FICTION SERIES
University of Kentucky
Lexington, Kentucky 40506-0027
U.S.A.

for my daughter
Aviva

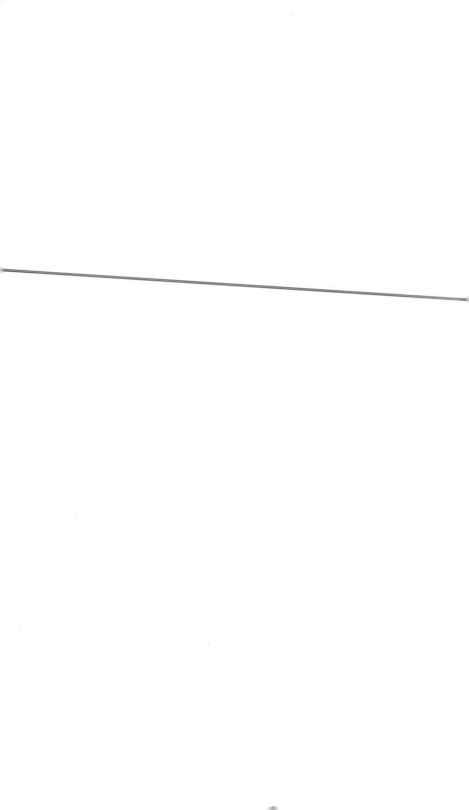

CONTENTS

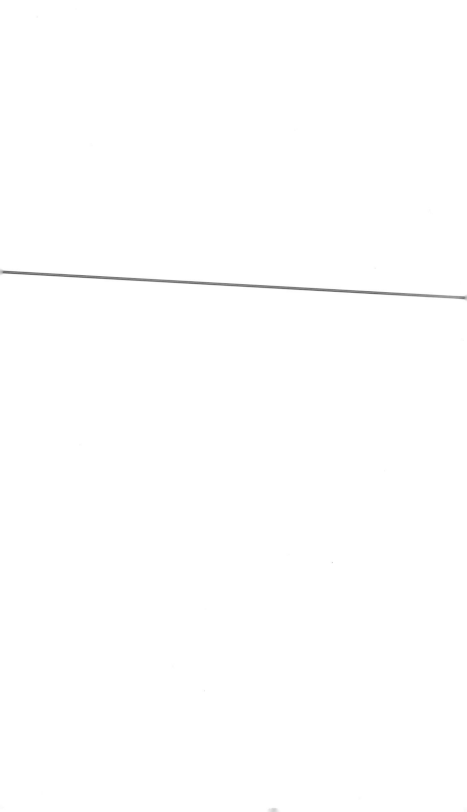

FIFTH SUNDAY

The church stood on a hill all to itself, at the intersection of Prospect and Maple. Opposite the broad, shallow steps and the three sets of double doors was a small ash-and-gravel parking lot, room for only a handful of cars; the minister and his assistants had reserved spaces, while the rest of the congregation used the side streets. Valerie's father always parked parallel to Prospect, nosing the sleek car down the steep brick road lined by abandoned houses and devil-strips overgrown to knee-level, weeds topped by sinister furred knobs.

Catercorner from the church was a park. It was everything a park should be: green, shaded, quiet. Stout black poles marked its perimeter at regular intervals, and strung between each pole were two chains, one at waist-level and another six inches from the ground. The park itself was segmented by two concrete paths that cut it on the diagonals, like a huge envelope. The paths seemed to serve no other purpose than help people walk through the park as quickly as possible: there were no animals, no vendors, no bandstand; Valerie could not remember ever seeing anyone sitting on the few chilly benches.

Valerie and the other young people of the church used the park as a shortcut to the all-night coffeehouse on East Exchange Street. "Max's Diner" was connected to a motel; each Sunday morning an exciting, bedraggled assortment of people could be found at the L-shaped counter. The waitress was called Vera; her upswept blonde hair resembled a fanciful antique urn. She was friendly; sometimes she even let them sit at the counter.

3

Usually they didn't have time to take a seat. Main Service began at eleven sharp; and though Sunday School was supposed to be over at 10:30, often their teacher, Mr. Brown, got so carried away that they had to resort to coughs and exaggerated glances at the clock before he caught on and let them loose—but not before a five minute lecture on obedience and diligence that made it nearly eleven by the time they got to Max's....

Of course, it hadn't always been like that. When she was little, Valerie wouldn't have dared slip off to anyplace as worldly as a diner. But now that she had been promoted to the Upper Sunday School, it was a matter of course to have a Mounds bar for furtive munching during church. The park hadn't always been a thoroughfare, either. Many, many years ago Valerie's mother had first been kissed there. She had been in the junior choir, and there was a boy among the tenors named John, with light brown eyes and long dark lashes. Choir rehearsals were on Tuesday evenings; before rehearsals the two of them, Valerie's mother and John, had taken to walking in the park. It was summer; the birds sat as if drugged in the trees. He touched her hand and then her cheek, and then he kissed her.

What was it like? "Nice—a kiss," was all her mother had to say about it. Valerie was fourteen and had never been kissed. It was impossible to imagine it ever happening. How did one go about it? Sure, there were plenty of boys around who wanted to—loud boys with scabs on their knuckles. No, she would have to like a boy before she let him kiss her. But as soon as she started to like someone, she got shy and tongue-tied whenever he tried to talk to her. What other choice did he have but to lose interest? No one can like a stone.

Church was the most glorious part of her existence. Her schoolmates she saw every day, in the halls or around the neighborhood—but when Sunday came, she would put on her best clothes and ride to the other side of the city. Deep familial traditions gave the church a varied congregation—people from all parts of town and all social and economic levels filled the dark waxed pews, so that once a week Valerie had friends who were different and met boys who played basketball in rival high schools. No wonder she scorned her classmates and looked forward to Sunday as if to a party.

She was not in the choir but in the junior ushers. Ever since she could remember, Valerie knew she would join one or the other. Whenever the choir stood up, their blue silk robes swaying slightly as they rocked to the beat, an amorphous yearning would surge in her, crystallizing to a single thought: *I can sing!* she would whisper, and bite her lip. Everyone knew, though, that most of the girls in the junior choir were "fast;" nowadays it was no honor to be associated with it.

Andrew was another reason for joining the usher board. He was the president. He was also the minister's son, and as such the undisputed leader of the male youth. He was very ugly—a pasty yellow color, and he wore his sandy hair in a short squarish afro, since it was too kinky to wear fuller. An overlarge lower lip pulled his mouth open slightly, exposing a row of widely-spaced teeth. His ears stood out and the lobes were covered with tiny indentations, as if someone had pricked them with a fork, like a pie shell. And he was blind in one eye. The story went that when he was ten he had been in a snowball fight; somebody threw a snowball with a stone in it. Valerie had to catch her breath whenever she thought of it. Imagine— you're playing outside with no other thought but fun when suddenly, from nowhere, a hard coldness slams into you—an arrow of ice—and when it's all over, you've lost half your sight. It must be horrible. It must be something you could never forget. Valerie found herself staring at Andrew. Of a mottled gray-blue color, both eyes were so beautifully vague that when the light struck them they seemed to disappear. If she watched closely she could pick up the slightly slower reaction of one iris, the minute flagging of the right eyelid when he looked sideways.

It endears him to me, Valerie said silently to herself as they drove home from church. After the car had crunched through the gravel driveway and she was safely in her room and had slipped off her patent-leather T-straps, she looked earnestly into the mirror and said, aloud this time: *It endears him to me.* She studied the tiny pearl earrings her parents had given her for graduation from grade school; she took them off, unscrewing the silver fastenings and locking them in the padded jewelry box. Andrew was seventeen. She had no chance.

She clutched to her passion like a pillow or a torch. On long Saturday afternoons she dreamed about the kiss to come— there was the park, there were the smoke-and-sky eyes to replace the light brown ones. Only when she daydreamed did Valerie experience the power of hope, a sense of luxurious apprehension.

One Saturday night the young people of the white Lutheran church one block over invited the black youth to see a movie on Martin Luther King. Valerie's mother dropped her off. It was still a little early, so she walked over to Prospect and stood for a while on the corner, looking down the hill.

This was not the choked, winding alley where her father parked--here the road fell straight and sharply into the city below. And she was on top of it, looking down. She really didn't know why she had walked to the church--maybe on the chance that the minister was inside working, and that Andrew might come walking out--maybe. But as she stood there looking down at the flushed sky and the indistinct trees clumped below it and below them, the tiny gray houses in the tiny gray streets, she felt a glow inside her chest--like a net with a brilliant fish struggling to escape--and she felt strong. Even the cool white steps of the church were not her equal.

She went back to the Lutheran church, where everyone had gathered in the basement. There were introductions, then the announcement for the start of the movie. Valerie was about to sit next to the aisle when Andrew came up and asked if she minded him sitting next to her. "Of course not," she said, and broke into a sweat behind her knees. She scooted over, trying to regain her composure. But Andrew would not wait for that. He plied her with questions—what kind of music did she like? Was she going to the high school track meet next week? He was sitting to her right, so the good eye could see every movement she made—still, whenever he said something, he turned so that they were face-to-face, the unresponsive eye giving him a vulnerable look. Then the lights went out. He crossed his legs and leaned back, throwing his left arm across the back of her chair; terrified, Valerie sat very still and tried to concentrate on the movie. From time to time Andrew would take away his arm, lean forward, and whisper in her ear; his comments were so hilarious that she could hardly keep from laughing out loud, and before the film was over she even managed a few witticisms of her own.

The next day was Fifth Sunday. Whenever there was a fifth Sunday in a month, the young people presided over the main service. They ushered, provided music, read the text from the Scriptures, passed the collection plate—even led the congregation in prayer for the sick and shut-in. The only thing they did not do was give the sermon. Valerie was so excited from the previous evening that she barely ate anything at breakfast. She had slept very little; and at seven she finally got up to press the knife-pleated white skirt. She hated their uniforms. The skirt was made from some synthetic material that stuck to her legs; the baggy white blouse was not cool at all. Besides, her period had started, which meant that she would have to wear the plastic-lined panties that made her feel like a baby in diapers.

Today, however, even that could not discourage her. Andrew would forego ushering to help at the altar, so today she could look at him as much as she pleased.

It was a hot, humid morning, and by 10:30 everyone looked limp and disgruntled. As on every Sunday when they ushered, the junior ushers did not go to Max's but convened in the small lounge off the main lobby. The decision who was going to "key" had to be made, and it was always a controversial one. There were four aisles to be covered. The side aisles had the least traffic and the windows. The right middle aisle was called the "key." Most of the people came down this aisle. The old, respected members had their regular seats in the front pews; the choir marched down this aisle and up into the chancel; all the fashionable middle class who'd come to show off their new clothes wanted seats in the middle section where they could be seen. The key usher had to remember where the regulars sat, get out of the way of the choir, gesture grandly to the bourgeoise's chosen pew, and take messages to the pulpit. Nobody wanted to be key.

Valerie was assigned aisle three. Of course she was glad she didn't have to key. But almost as many people came down her aisle as down the other middle aisle. It was strange how people always streamed toward the middle of anyplace. At the supermarket they fought for a parking space in the thick of all the other cars; after church in the lobby or on the steps they gravitated toward the largest groups, squeezing through the outer fringe to get a better angle on the discussion in the inner circle. But at least—even if she didn't have a window—she had an unobstructed view of the altar. Except when the congregation stood up to sing, she could see Andrew clearly. He wore a light blue suit with a yellow shirt just a shade brighter than his skin. He looked self-confident, compassionate. He caught her glance and smiled.

The doors opened and people poured in. Valerie was shy of them. They were always in a hurry to be seated and never really looked at her. Today, though, she felt she was getting through it fairly well—although once when there was a crush of people, she had trouble with an old man whose cane kept getting jammed between the pews and some woman in a pink silk hat squeezed past Valerie impatiently, the thick scent of her perfume trailing her like fame itself. Valerie's stomach was growling; she hoped no one could hear it.

Sunlight bowled through the vaulted windows; sweat stood out in delicate beaded patterns on the powdered brows of the women; the cardboard fans in the hands of the junior choir members flitted at an amazing rate, like small scared birds. Valerie felt the dampness under her arms, between her shoulder blades, inside the plastic pants. Her stockings felt like they had been dragged in wet sand—in fact she itched all over, and she kept shifting her weight from one foot to the other and adjusting her white gloves. *I'll stick it out until this song is over and then I'll leave the floor,* she thought; but when the congregation had regained their seats Valerie felt that would look too conspicuous; so she decided to wait until the responsive reading was over. She tried concentrating on a sunbeam that bisected the small table where the gleaners were arrayed. *After the responsive reading,* she thought, *the little girls in their white robes will march up to the altar, and each one will take a gleaner and pass it from row to row, and each person will take out a dime or a nickel and drop it in the slot...*Valerie thought of the sound all those coins clinking against glass would make. The sunbeam had separated into tiny glowing dots, and there were particles of dust suspended between the spots—the sun glancing off of all that silver made her dizzy....

How cool it had become suddenly, and a breeze too! It was a relief to be able to take her mind off her problems. At any rate, she was glad the weather had broken. Now she was lying in a hammock on the back porch with a tall cool glass of punch beside her. As she rocked back and forth, the wind—no, no more than a breath, a zephyr!—lifted her hair to dry her forehead, then dropped each strand gently back into place. Faraway the doorbell rang. She heard her mother's voice, then footsteps growing louder and the screen door slamming; she swooned in delicious anticipation, and then Andrew was beside her with a cool hand for her forehead and a gaze of tender solicitude radiating from the watery depths of his eyes....

Why did she feel so terrible all of a sudden, and why had the sun come back? For a moment there was nothing but a piercing whiteness, and Valerie felt as if she were floating—but badly, in jerks and bobs. Someone was whispering below her...what were they saying? *She must have fainted.*

No! Valerie tried to lift her head but only succeeded in looking down the length of her own body, which was stiff as a board. Several men were carrying her down the aisle. The service had stopped; she lifted her head again, and this time saw the choir's and the minister's startled faces suspended at the far end of the aisle. Then they were gone.

She was laid out on a couch in the lounge and a fat woman in white with a businesslike manner stuck something under her nose. An electric shock jolted her to the base of her spine. After the coolness and the dream of Andrew, this nausea! She felt wounded in her soul. More than anything she was ashamed.

Faces mooned above her and hands undid her collar, rubbed her wrists. None of their administrations did anything but agitate her still further, and she was about to tell them so (if she could only get her mouth to cooperate), when a woman Valerie did not recognize appeared at the foot of the couch and leaned over her. The woman made no attempt to help; she looked Valerie up and down with a hard cool stare and said, "Who knows? Maybe she's pregnant."

Valerie sputtered, struggling onto her elbows, but the nurse held her down. "It's not true!" she gasped and tried to get up again. The circle of faces closed in on her, whispering soothing things she could not understand. The woman had disappeared. No one would tell Valerie her name, though she thrashed and pleaded.

Valerie's parents had arrived. Her father stood awkwardly to one side as her mother knelt beside the couch and looked at her with large, troubled eyes. Valerie barely noticed them; she was thinking of the woman spitting that word over her like a pronouncement: *pregnant.* Well, the bitch wouldn't get away with it. There weren't that many people in this church she didn't know—she'd find out who she was. She'd make them tell. Bitch. She'd find her. She'd find her.

THE ZULUS

Like their name, they soared on the dark edges of adventure and superstition—young men on heavy Japanese machines, custom-made leather jackets rippling over their chests and across the backs, at the shoulders the biker's name and their trademark, a flaming spear and a skull, stitched in silver and crimson. They poured through the streets of a dying city, honking and shouting to the uninitiated behind curtains. *Where were you when the lights went out?* they sang, *in Buffalo, Pittsburgh, Cleveland, Chi-town, Motown, Gary Indiana*...for they had been to all these places which belched along the glittery soiled neckline of North America.

They were high-school age, though some had dropped out. Parents warned their daughters away: *if nothing else, think of your family.* The members of the High School Honor Society officially shunned them. Girls tittered nervously whenever one of them sauntered down the corridor.

Which was why, when I heard that Swoop had asked Caroline Mosley to the Prom, I laughed. Actually, I snorted. It was absurd. His real name was Leander Swope, but everybody called him Swoop because that's the sound the basketball net made whenever he was there for the handoff. Like a kiss, his shots were perfect. Swoop! The crowd went wild.

Leander Swope may have been a thing of beauty on the court, but in classes he was just another beetle-browed athlete, dim-witted and sullen. Rumor had it that the two diagonal gouges

10

on his left cheek were dug there by a girl's fingernails as she tried to defend herself. But I knew those scars were the marks of dishonor—the brand for those brave enough to undergo the initiation into the Zulus.

And Caroline? Caroline was beyond reproach. When everyone in fourth grade had to give a demonstration speech, Caroline brought in a mop and dustcloths and explained how one cleaned a house. As the youngest daughter of a broken home, I guess she had had lots of practice. She was dimpled and was fun to be around; although she had lots of boyfriends, they all spoke well of her. The girls liked her, too.

"The men in this town are spoiled," she would say. "Somehow they got it into their heads that they're a blessing to us all, and they run around with their noses in the stratosphere. Have you ever heard of a guy expecting the girl to call him up before? They'll stand there bold as day and scribble their phone number on a greasy slip of paper. And when another girl tries to steal him, he expects you to fight for him! Look at them—a bunch of the sorriest mangy dogs around. When are these gals going to do something for themselves? Look at the women in this town—aren't they some of the prettiest women you've ever seen?" We looked around. It was true.

And when her father discovered Black Power and moved into an apartment where he could put up his H. Rap Brown posters and entertain turbanned sisters under black lights, Caroline went on as if nothing had happened. And we followed her lead. After all, we knew nothing about divorces and too many children. We were friends, but we never spoke much about personal matters.

So when I heard about Swoop and Caroline, I didn't ask her if it was true. I waited...and when Prom night came, watched with the others in amazement as the band opened with a fanfare of saxes and Swoop and Caroline appeared in matching baby blue, looking like the plastic dolls on a wedding cake.

It was not to be comprehended, but we didn't have time to ponder. We had to pack for college. We were already in the world of Shetland sweaters and meal tickets.

The summer after our first year at college, we saw Caroline again. She was working at Pittsburgh Plate Glass; Swoop had lost his job at the potato chip factory. She hadn't changed at all—she laughed at our descriptions of the "educated turkeys" we'd dated and gave us an update on the exploits of our former Homecoming queen. She giggled as she told us how her mother nearly caught her and Lee buck naked on the leather E-Z chair in the basement. We had all lost our virginity that year, so we tried not to make a big deal of it, but inside we were shocked. It was something you didn't talk about.

In August the announcement came: a garden wedding. DeeDee, Caroline's older sister, met three of us in a movie and offered the services of her boyfriend—a tall dark-skinned dude with a diamond stud in one ear—for driving us to the wedding, since it was on the north side of town. DeeDee was what we called "fast." She had very fine features and slightly slanted black eyes set in a heart-shaped face the color of pale coffee, and it seems everything she wore was calculated to hide her beauty--she tacked on false eyelashes and fake clover-leafed "beauty marks;" she dyed her hair a different shade every month (this time it was the color of sherry) and poked heavy gold hoops through her ears.

On the day of the wedding a blossom-white convertible spun into the driveway and out he unfolded, long limbs resplendent in royal blue with a lavender silk shirt. He arranged us with all due courtesy in the leather upholstery and spun off again. After a year with no opportunity to dress up, we had outdone ourselves—there were even white gloves tucked in the side pockets of our purses. But our hair! DeeDee's friend's convertible had no mercy. In collective dismay we felt our upsweep tugged loose, the curls swept from a pageboy, a silk gardenia flapping indignantly on the last bobby pin.

The garden was nothing more than a hastily mown lawn. Folding chairs had been set up in the back yard and the side lot, surrounded by a latticed fence, bordered on a dead-end street. The path between the folding chairs led up to a wicker arbor laced with vines and studded with blue carnations.

We took our places on the side designated for "friends of the bride" and waited for the music. A quarter of an hour passed. People began to whisper: Lee was mad because he couldn't invite his motorcycle buddies; someone had forgotten the marriage license; Lee was inside watching baseball on T.V. and wouldn't come out until the game was over. From the window behind us could be heard muted voices, interrupted by sporadic cheering. Poor Caroline! What an ending for the most admired girl in the city, one who owed it to herself to do better. And for what— Love? Here, in a backyard where roses drooped, babies squawled, bees attacked and here and there a dandelion showed its impertinent proletarian head? No, it wasn't possible.

The voices stopped and the mothers—Lee's in pale blue and Caroline's in yellow—marched down the aisle and seated themselves in the front row. The bridegroom and the minister appeared at the arbor; Leander looked surprisingly handsome in a light blue tuxedo with a cream-colored ruffled shirt. The beautiful, whorish DeeDee skimmed by, followed by an entourage of blue silks and unfamiliar faces, concluding with the intolerably cute ring bearer with his plump pillow.

A white cloth was rolled out, and in its wake came Caroline—the old Caroline, with a spray of blue and white flowers and the dimples held in check. Her father, aware of his uselessness, tried to look inconspicuous. When the Lohengrin—which had been assaulting us from a stereo at the back of the house—stopped, the babies started up again. In a short while it was over, and without having heard a word we made our way to the adjoining yard where the tables were stacked with plates of ham and chicken.

There was nothing left to say. It was done. Caroline presented a dimpled cheek and looked genuinely happy. We looked for a hostess but none was introduced.

Some guests had already lined up for a second piece of cake when a low-pitched noise grew above the general hum of voices. It was a fuzzy rumble that sharpened as it drew nearer, stopping all conversation, inspiring even the babies to silence. When it seemed the sound could come no nearer, the first of them appeared, helmets flashing the gilt insignia of the Zulus, a spear and a skull. They drove up the dead-end street and parked their bikes along the fence, clustering in a dark glittering knot. Swoop greeted them with a shout, and they clapped him on the back. They wouldn't come in but they would have some cake—which Swoop passed over the fence in crumbling chunks while Caroline, a rose among thorns, stood by smiling.

THE SPRAY PAINT KING

When did you first take to the streets? Bitch with pad and pencil, doodling cocks in the margin while digging at me with that cool soft voice. *What criteria determined your choice of buildings?* Blue eyes trained on some far-off point as if she were driving her BMW on the Autobahn. *Why do you use black paint?* Blonde hair crimped like a statue's. A down home German girl.

I walk over to the window, casually, and stare down at the Rhine. I know she wonders just how black I am. She wonders how many sessions before she can ask me about my ancestry. *Ach Mädchen*—when I see you sitting on that straight-back chair, ankles crossed and pad balanced on those waffly thighs, I imagine you as my private stenographer. Taking down all my pearls.

If she would look a little further than my crinkly hair, if she would glance over my shoulder, I would point out the Cologne Cathedral, rising from the glass and steel *Hauptbahnhof* like a medieval missile launch; I would show her the three blackened arches of the Hohenzollern Bridge and, further to the right, upriver from Old St. Alban's, the bare metal stripe that's the Köln-Deutz Autobridge, then the little tower at the tip of the harbor whose name I've forgotten and...there it is. Severin Bridge. Saint Severin of the eleventh century, whose bones lie boxed in gold in a church on the south side of the city.

I'll call her Severin, that bitch who calls herself my psychiatrist. Though her ID might show otherwise: Doctor Severin.

14

How I feel about Diana, she asks. Why don't you guess for a while. Gives you something to do when you're lying alone between the frottee bedsheets, exhausted from your own pleasure but unable to sleep. (I've watched you squirm in that hard chair. I've seen you secretly sniffing your fingers as you put away pad and pencil in the desk drawer.) And if you still can't sleep, you can type up your notes. I see it now: Case History of the Spray Paint King.

*

Dr. Severin has decided I should keep my journal private until I think I am finished. My first entry shocked her (did you cream in your panties, my bride, my Edeltraut? Did I catch you right?) *Seventeen and already asocial.* She thinks she can take the wind out of my sails. He will tire of these juvenile insults, she thinks, when no one is there to read them. She has provided me with a list of questions. Why did you drop out of high school? When did you join a motorcycle gang? How did you meet Diana? What satisfaction does defacing public buildings give you?

I am forced to do your bidding, but it is not easy. So many questions! I'll need an outline to answer them all:

I. Background
   A. Family
   B. Sexual experiences

II. Onset of Criminal/Artistic Activities
   A. My friends above the river
   B. Concrete vs. stressed steel
   C. Flick of the wrist

This, then, Lady Bockwurst, is for you. Take it in memory of me and the deeds I have wrought upon this blighted city, scab on the banks of the Rhine.

*

When I was ten, my mother sent me to the cellar to haul coal. I was frightened, and the scuttle banged my knee several times in my haste to escape; but by the third trip, I gathered courage to linger. Under the flickering light of the naked bulb swinging, the coal gleamed dimly, like wax, in huge craggy mounds. All that coal dust I had inhaled every winter, all the tenements dulled with soot and the chilling rain and the sky like an iron glove, all that dusty and gingery despair settling on the skin like grit—blackness undiluted, one hundred percent.

But years went by before I unzipped my pants for the first time. I didn't know what would come next—just that it felt good. I couldn't stop, even when my spine threatened to sink between my knees. Then something broke inside me and splattered against the wall of coal. Now I'm going to die, I thought, watching it grow translucent, darken to a gray jelly.

*

As such, Diana's nothing special. But the way she walked as if her head doesn't know what her body is doing...and what it does is sensational. Not that she's a knockout. Her breasts are average but she's so slim that they're...well, *there*. And legs like a young boy, legs that don't stop. And a round trim ass. She wears corduroy pants, tight, in orange and pink and lilac; she looks like a tree and the fruit on it.

Diana hung out at the Hi-Fly, our penny-arcade on the east bank. Everyone in the gang was afraid to touch her unless they were high—then sometimes they'd take her for a ride across the Autobahn bridge. Every time she came back, she looked as if she were drowning.

But the oddest thing about Diana, what made me start paying attention to her, was that she read books. Philosophy, anthropology—things like that. She'd sit at a table, a flair pen between her lacquered fingernails, underlining. I watched her several nights before I went over. The guys liked to kid her, asking her if Sigmund Freud was her great-granddaddy, stuff like that. But when I sat with Diana, I didn't ask her anything. I didn't even talk. I just watched her read. I believe she understood what she read, because when she was reading was the only time her head and body seemed to come together.

It got so I'd sit there until the Hi-Fly closed, watching the flair pen move under her fingers. I drank one mango juice after another; watching pink ink move through the words. (You wouldn't understand, Dr. Severin; how peaceful I felt.) Then one night—the sky was a deep, tricky blue—Diana finished a book. I had never seen her finish one before. I waited for her to fish the next one out of her handbag; but she clicked the pen shut and threw the paperback on the table. I stared at the cover, something about the phenomenology of space. The author had a French name.

"Let's go for a ride," she said, standing up. I nodded and went for my bike.

We rode every bridge over the river that night, all eight of them. We roared around the square at Neumarkt four times. We teased the prostitutes on Weidengasse and the bums at the *Hauptbahnhof*. Somewhere in Ehrenfeld we got lost and wandered around through the deserted underpasses until we stumbled onto a familiar street and started back into town. Swinging past the radio station, we saw a man in a three-piece suit practicing turns on roller skates. His briefcase lay propped neatly against a balustrade.

"All the white buildings," Diana whispered, and when I turned around she had that drowned look.

And finally the dingy spires of the cathedral, spotlit to remind us all where we were, the great *Köln am Rhein*, home of toilet water and pale bitter beer.

*

Anonymous benefactors send me sketch pads and charcoals. Yesterday a packet from Zurich—precision drafting pens and an arsenal of pastels. I distributed them among the guys on my corridor. As if, after painting the town, I would doodle on a slip of paper.

The only decent gift came from a Martin Tauber, Dr. phil., Free University of Berlin. "You keep good company," he wrote inside the front cover. Lithographs by Picasso. I'm not sure what he meant, Dr. phil. Tauber—I'm not academic. But the book's not bad. A series of sketches of a bull caught my eye. First Picasso draws a bull in every detail—cock, balls, muscles and all. In the next picture, the bull has lost his muscles, but he's still a damned fine beast. Next he loses his hooves and eyes and the tail's just a swooping line. Then he sports a branch with two leaves sticking to it instead of a cock. By the time Picasso's finished there's only two or three ink strokes on the page. But it's still a bull. Inside the front cover Dr. Tauber had also pasted this newspaper clipping about my sprayings:

The young artist's style is reminiscent of Picasso in austerity of line, of Matisse in fantasy and social comment.

The bitterness, however, the relentless scrutiny of what we so vainly call civilization, the hopelessness which pervades his work, without coquetterie nor call for pathos— these qualities are all his own. He is, so to speak, his generation's appointed messenger.

Bingo. The Big Time. Razzmatazz.

*

Certainly Dr. Severin considers the possibility that I might, one day, pull her onto the shrink-couch: she considers the possibility with a mixture of thrilling curiosity and propitious dread.

There's a term for me—*quadroon*. Every time I say the word, I think of pale chewy cookies and laugh. I'm what girls call a treat—*ein Leckerbissen*. Gray eyes with a slight tilt. Flaring nostrils on a sharp nose. A large, clear brow. Women either shy from me on the street or linger, smiling. Men's eyes narrow.

The Negro blood is more prominent in me, in fact, than in my mother. From a very light baby with a cheesy complexion, I darkened during kindergarten. It began at the ears and descended with frightening rapidity to the neck (pale coffee). Lines appeared in my palms like lemon juice scribblings held over a flame. The hair, so fine and wispy, crinkled. The pink cheeks of my classmates huffed and puffed: *Negerlein, Negerlein.*

My mother, conversely, lightened as she aged. When I was younger she reminded me of some magnificent bird of prey, tall and goldenskinned with an aquiline nose set into the flat strong bones of her face. Her plucked brows perch like talons above her eyes which are hazel and wide apart. She wears her thick hair tied back with a ribbon, like a girl.

But way back in Aachen, during the last snow-whipped days of 1945, my grandmother—when she studied the caramel-colored face of her new daughter—had been in despair. She had never set eyes on a black person before the soldier from the land of chewing gum and grapefruit spoke to her in his elastic voice. He gave her chocolate bars and promised to return. Then the British arrived, and she packed her things, walking eastward towards her hometown Dresden, pleading aid from military convoys—the swarthy baby helped. By the time my mother learned to walk, they had gotten as far as the border

18

of the Soviet Occupied Zone and were turned back, placed on a U.S. Army truck headed west. A Negro M.P. was loading the refugees; my mother began to cry when his hands reached for her; she did not stop until, smiling, he drew on white gloves.

*

My father works construction; his idea of recreation is to take a streetcar to an unfamiliar quarter of town and to walk his family through it, pointing out buildings which are in need of repair or soon to be torn down. Once, when I was eleven, we took the streetcar as far as Chlodwigplatz; we got out near St. Severin's Gate with its little terracotta tower and strolled through the cobblestone streets. My parents held hands and laughed at my Lancelot-like attempts to spar with the neighborhood dogs. It was one of those September evenings when the sky is rinsed clean and hot, a light that makes you feel exhilarated and melancholic, in the same breath. To the right, between crenelated facades, the Rhine glittered like an alchemist's greed; all the sparrows of late summer swooped to the lowest branches and blinked at the earthbound pitingly. We turned down Dreikönigsstrasse, towards the river, and when we could go no further, my father stopped and pointed a blunt finger at the pale green Severin Bridge.

"Like a bird's long dream," he said, "a tribute to modern engineering." And with a proud sigh: "I helped build it...for three years of my life."

The next day I looked it up in my *Kinderlexikon*. Span, 300 meters. Steel box girders braced by three sets of cables passed over the top of the A-shaped tower located near the east bank. I went to the public library to find out more details. *Köln— History of a Modern City*. Five men were buried in one of the cement pilings...

I ran to my mother and found her bent over the bathtub, rinsing sheets. "How could they?" I asked.

"How could they what?" she countered.

"Leave those men to die!"

"Don't tell me," she began, slapping sheets against the side of the tub, "you've been reading those westerns again." Then she saw the book clutched to my chest, and her hands ceased their convulsive wringing.

"Who are you talking about?" she asked.

"Josef Breit, Mathias Metzger, Winfried—"

"Not their names!" She caught herself shouting, spoke softer. "I know." The afternoon sun splashing through the blinds and across her face turned her eyes pale gold.

"They fell into a hole while pouring concrete. The others kept pouring..."

For a moment my mother hesitated, her hands quiet in the water. Then her face hardened. "That's your father's territory," she replied. "Ask him." Bending over, she attacked the laundry with renewed energy, wringing the sheets.

"What did you want us to do," Dad said, leaning back in his armchair, "stop production and dig them out?"

*

Yesterday the street cleaners, under orders from the city, prepared to erase one of my sprayings with XR-3, the chemical abrasive concocted to eliminate political graffiti left over from the student movement. The spraying in question, nicknamed "Space Flower" by the press, blooms on the facade of a prominent bank; this plant with its dagger stamens and cone-shaped appendages arcs in perfect imitation of a statue poised beside it, a bronze replica of the bank's first president.

The street cleaners moved in early—around 6 a.m.—hoping to avoid a confrontation. But news had leaked; already grouped around the statue, in a neat but impenetrable mass, were the apprentices from the art academy, many non-partisan radicals and some Young Socialists.

Supposedly no one said a word. A fine cold rain began. After a few minutes, the cleaners turned on their heels and drove away.

*

Diana comes to visit; she wears a blue dress and looks exhausted. I wonder what Dr. Severin has been telling her.

"I knew it was you," she blurts out. "I knew as soon as I saw which buildings you picked. The newspapers. The radio station. The sides of tenements, concrete retaining walls. All white."

Getting the spray cans, easy. The clerk at Hertie's department store couldn't take his eyes off Diana's butt. The youth center ran out of black paint while decorating their float for the *Karneval* parade. But how to explain the drives at night, my bike lubed and polished for the trip? How explain the building calling with its face blank as snow awaiting defilement? Natural canvasses.

"It started that night, didn't it?"

We had stopped in the middle of the Severin Bridge; I cut the motor. The bridge was too high for us to hear the movement of the Rhine but the wind hummed through the cables; it was almost like listening to the water. Five men are buried in this stanchion, I told her, staring into the glittering lights. I recited their names, I repeated what my mother and father had said. She listened, and when I turned around her eyes were gliding from one side of my face to the other as if I were one of her books. She took my head in her hands; her palms burned but her fingertips were like ice. She kissed me. I was twisted half-backwards on my motorcycle—an awkward position—but we did not get off.

Today Diana looks straight into my eyes. The room is brightly lit, and the greenish wallpaper makes me shiver, despite the overheated iron radiators underneath the barred windows. Rush hour traffic roars outside of this "detention home for youthful offenders."

"Why did you paint the Madonna?"

Can I explain what itch built up inside me, how I tried to ignore it at first and *act responsibly*, then learned to welcome its presence and nurture it, prime it, hone the vague desires to a single, jubilant swoop, one vibrant gesture?

"I didn't paint her," I replied. "She painted herself."

The Madonna. When I had finished I just stood there, looking at her—I would have stood there all night, the stars shone so soft and cool. I didn't give a shit about anything, except for that picture. I didn't budge, even when a pair of young lovers strolled around the corner. For a moment we stood quietly and gazed at her. Then the woman pointed: "The police!"—and I bolted.

"I always thought..." Why does Diana look down at her lap, Diana whose eyes were reputed to batter the most lascivious suitor to a bale of twigs? "I always figured..."—a coy swoop of eyelashes—"you drew her after me. You know—tits and ass." She laughs disparagingly.

That's why the dress. Blue, too. Ah, Diana—again you are right, but it means so little. The Madonna is my masterpiece. The councilman in charge of education (a member of the Christian Democratic Party) has called her "the product of a sick and

21

filthy mind." What do you think, Diana? Am I sick or are you just beautiful?

*

My mother comes every day and cries. She says it's all her fault. She says she knows how it feels to be always stared at and never loved, how one is never comfortable except in the smallest of spaces, at the stove or bent over a tub of suds. She raves. When it gets too much I play out the fantasy I had as a child; I am sent down to the cellar for coal. While I am filling the scuttle, the Americans drop the Big Bomb. When I come upstairs again, I am the only German left in the whole country—all because I have to haul coal when other little boys are outside playing.

Dr. Severin will read this and say: "The coal saves you—your black blood." And when I paint I'm spraying blood on the walls or semen, a fascinating example of reverse projection. She wants to ease me back into society; she will tell me I have a talent I mustn't squander.

*

First there is the blue of the air as they fall, open-mouthed, open-eyed, toward a deeper blue. Then the red of impact, the stunned blow as their mouths fill and capillaries pop. And then, for the longest kind of time, the black before death and then the black of dying, the black of metal before it is painted sea green and the black of sea green metal against the sun, an unfinished web. But when most people have forgotten, when those men become no more than a macabre joke at a party, or the niggling conscience of an engineer as he drives to work, they will float up out of the stanchion and through the rain-slick streets of Cologne, looking for a place to tell their story. The newspapers will scoff; the radio station will shrug. Their walls are clean.

The city stands in concrete snow and even the cathedral's turned white overnight. Oh citizens who have forgotten, I was there to remind you, I put the stain back on the wall—no outraged slogan, no incoherent declaration of love, but a gesture both graceful and treacherous, a free fall ending in disaster—among the urgent scrawls of history, a mere flick of the wrist.

SECOND-HAND MAN

Virginia couldn't stand it when someone tried to shorten her name—like *Ginny*, for example. But James Evans didn't. He set his twelve-string guitar down real slow.

"Miss Virginia," he said, "you're a fine piece of woman."

Seemed he'd been asking around. Knew everything about her. Knew she was bold and proud and didn't cotton to no silly niggers. Vir-gin-ee-a he said, nice and slow. Almost Russian, the way he said it. Right then and there she knew this man was for her.

He courted her just inside a year, came by nearly every day. First she wouldn't see him for more than half an hour at a time. She'd send him away; he knew better than to try to force her. Another fellow did that once—kept coming by when she said she had other things to do. She told him he do it once more, she'd be waiting at the door with a pot of scalding water to teach him some manners. Did, too. Fool didn't believe her— she had the pot waiting on the stove and when he came up those stairs, she was standing in the door. He took one look at her face and turned and ran. He was lucky those steps were so steep. She only got a little piece of his pant leg.

No, James knew his stuff. He'd come on time and stay till she told him he needed to go.

She'd met him out at Summit Beach one day. In the Twenties, that was the place to go on hot summer days! Clean yellow sand all around the lake, and an amusement park that ran from morning to midnight. She went there with a couple of girl friends. They were younger than her and a little silly. But they

23

were sweet. Virginia was nineteen then. "High time," everyone used to say to her, but she'd just lift her head and go on about her business. She weren't going to marry just any old Negro. He had to be perfect.

There was a man who was chasing her around about that time, too. Tall dark Negro—Sterling Williams was his name. Pretty as a panther. Married, he was. Least that's what everyone said. Left a wife in Washington, D.C. A little crazy, the wife— poor Sterling was trying to get a divorce.

Well, Sterling was at Summit Beach that day, too. He followed Virginia around, trying to buy her root beer. Everybody loved root beer that summer. Root beer and vanilla ice cream— the Boston Cooler. But she wouldn't pay him no mind. People said she was crazy—Sterling was the best catch in Akron, they said.

"Not for me," Virginia said. "I don't want no second-hand man."

But Sterling wouldn't give up. He kept buying root beers and having to drink them himself.

Then she saw James. He'd just come up from Tennessee, working his way up on the riverboats. Folks said his best friend had been lynched down there and he turned his back on the town and said he was never coming back. Well, when she saw this cute little man in a straw hat and a twelve-string guitar under his arm, she got a little flustered. Her girlfriends whispered around to find out who he was, but she acted like she didn't even see him.

He was the hit of Summit Beach. Played that twelve-string guitar like a devil. They'd take off their shoes and sit on the beach toward evening. All the girls loved James. "Oh, Jimmy," they'd squeal, "play us a *loooove* song!" He'd laugh and pick out a tune:

> *I'll give you a dollar if you'll come out tonight*
> *If you'll come out tonight,*
> *If you'll come out tonight.*
> *I'll give you a dollar if you'll come out tonight*
> *And dance by the light of the moon.*

Then the girls would giggle. "Jimmy," they screamed, "you outta be 'shamed of yourself!" He'd sing the second verse then:

I danced with a girl with a hole in her stockin',
And her heel kep' a-rockin',
And her heel kep' a-rockin';
I danced with a girl with a hole in her stockin',
And we danced by the light of the moon.

Then they'd all priss and preen their feathers and wonder which would be best—to be in fancy clothes and go on being courted by these dull factory fellows, or to have a hole in their stockings and dance with James.

Virginia never danced. She sat a bit off to one side and watched them make fools of themselves.

Then one night near season's end, they were all sitting down by the water, and everyone had on sweaters and was in a foul mood because the cold weather was coming and there wouldn't be no more parties. Someone said something about hating having the good times end, and James struck up a nice and easy tune, looking across the fire straight at Virginia:

As I was lumb'ring down de street,
Down de street, down de street,
A han'some gal I chanced to meet,
Oh, she was fair to view!

I'd like to make dat gal my wife,
Gal my wife, gal my wife.
I'd be happy all my life
If I had her by me.

She knew he was the man. She'd known it a long while, but she was just biding her time. He called on her the next day. She said she was busy canning peaches. He came back the day after. They sat on the porch and watched the people go by. He didn't talk much, except to say her name like that:

"Vir-gin-ee-a," he said, "you're a mighty fine woman."

She sent him home a little after that. He showed up again a week later. She was angry at him and told him she didn't have time for playing around. But he'd brought his twelve-string guitar, and he said he'd been practicing all week just to play a couple of songs for her. She let him in then and made him sit on the stool while she sat on the porch swing. He sang the first song. It was a floor thumper.

There is a gal in our town,
She wears a yellow striped gown,
And when she walks the streets aroun',
The hollow of her foot makes a hole in the ground.

Ol' folks, young folks, cl'ar the kitchen,
Ol' folks, young folks, cl'ar the kitchen,
Ol' Virginny never tire.

She got a little mad then, but she knew he was baiting her. Seeing how much she would take. She knew he wasn't singing about her, and she'd already heard how he said her name. It was time to let the dog in out of the rain, even if he shook his wet all over the floor. So she leaned back and put her hands on her hips, real slow.

"I just *know* you ain't singing about me."

"Virginia," he replied, with a grin would've put Rudolph Valentino to shame, "I'd *never* sing about you that way."

He pulled a yellow scarf out of his trouser pocket. Like melted butter it was, with fringes.

"I saw it yesterday and thought how nice it would look against your skin," he said.

That was the first present she ever accepted from a man. Then he sang his other song:

I'm coming, I'm coming!
Virginia, I'm coming to stay.
Don't hold it agin' me
For running away.

And if I can win ya,
I'll never more roam,
I'm coming Virginia,
My dixie land home.

She was gone for him. Not like those girls on the beach: she had enough sense left to crack a joke or two. "You saying I look like the state of Virginia?" she asked, and he laughed. But she was gone.

She didn't let him know it, though, not for a long while. Even when he asked her to marry him, eight months later, he was trembling and thought she just might refuse out of some woman's whim. No, he courted her proper. Every day for a little while. They'd sit on the porch until it got too cold and then they'd sit in the parlor with two or three bright lamps on. Her mother and father were glad Virginia'd found a beau, but they weren't taking any chances. Everything had to be proper.

He got down, all trembly, on one knee and asked her to be his wife. She said yes. There's a point when all this dignity and stuff get in the way of Destiny. He kept on trembling; he didn't believe her.

"What?" he said.

"I said yes," Virginia answered. She was starting to get angry. Then he saw that she meant it, and he went into the other room to ask her father for her hand in marriage.

But people are too curious for their own good, and there's some things they never need to know, but they're going to find them out one way or the other. James had come all the way up from Tennessee and that should have been far enough, but he couldn't hide that snake any more. It just crawled out from under the rock when it was good and ready.

The snake was Jeremiah Morgan. Some fellows from Akron had gone off for work on the riverboats, and some of these fellows had heard about James. That twelve-string guitar and straw hat of his had made him pretty popular. So, story got to town that James had a baby somewhere. And joined up to this baby—but long dead and buried—was a wife.

Virginia had been married six months when she found out from sweet-talking, side-stepping Jeremiah Morgan who never liked her no-how after she'd laid his soul to rest one night when he'd taken her home from a dance. (She always carried a brick in her purse—no man could get the best of her!)

Jeremiah must have been the happiest man in Akron the day he found out. He found it out later than most people—things like that have a way of circulating first among those who know how to keep it from spreading to the wrong folks—then when the gossip's gotten to everyone else, it's handed over to the one who knows what to do with it.

"Ask that husband of your'n what else he left in Tennessee besides his best friend," was all Jeremiah said at first.

No no-good Negro like Jeremiah Morgan could make Virginia beg for information. She wouldn't bite.

"I ain't got no need for asking my husband nothing," she said, and walked away. She was going to choir practice.

He stood where he was, yelled after her like any old common person. "Mrs. Evans always talking about being Number 1! It looks like she's Number 2 after all."

Her ears burned from the shame of it. She went on to choir practice and sang her prettiest; and straight when she was back home she asked:

"What's all this number two business?"

James broke down and told her the whole story—how he'd been married before, when he was seventeen, and his wife dying in childbirth and the child not quite right because of being blue when it was born. And how when his friend was strung up he saw no reason for staying. And how when he met Virginia, he found out pretty quick what she'd done to Sterling Williams and that she'd never have no second-hand man, and he had to have her, so he never said a word about his past.

She took off her coat and hung it in the front closet. She unpinned her hat and set it in its box on the shelf. She reached in the back of the closet and brought out his hunting rifle and the box of bullets. She didn't see no way out but to shoot him.

"Put that down!" he shouted. "I love you!"

"You were right not to tell me," she said, "because I sure as sin wouldn't have married you. I don't want you now."

"Virginia!" he said. He was real scared. "How can you shoot me down like this?"

No, she couldn't shoot him when he stood there looking at her with those sweet brown eyes, telling her how much he loved her.

"You have to sleep sometime," she said, and sat down to wait.

He didn't sleep for three nights. He knew she meant business. She sat up in their best chair with the rifle across her lap, but he wouldn't sleep. He sat at the table and told her over and over that he loved her and he hadn't known what else to do at the time.

"When I get through killing you," she told him, "I'm going to write to Tennessee and have them send that baby up here. It won't do, farming a child out to any relative with an extra plate."

She held onto that rifle. Not that he would have taken it from her—not that that would've saved him. No, the only thing would've saved him was running away. But he wouldn't run either.

Sitting there, Virginia had lots of time to think. He was afraid of what she might do, but he wouldn't leave her, either. Some of what he was saying began to sink in. He had lied, but that was the only way to get her—she could see the reasoning behind that. And except for that, he was perfect. It was hardly like having a wife before at all. And the baby—anyone could see the marriage wasn't meant to be anyway.

On the third day about midnight, she laid down the rifle.

"You will join the choir and settle down instead of plucking on that guitar anytime anyone drop a hat," she said. "And we will write to your aunt in Tennessee and have that child sent up here." Then she put the rifle back in the closet.

The child never made it up to Ohio—it had died a month before Jeremiah ever opened his mouth. That hit James hard. He thought it was his fault and all, but Virginia made him see the child was sick and was probably better off with its Maker than it would be living out half a life.

James made a good tenor in the choir. The next spring, Virginia had her first baby and they decided to name her Belle. That's French for beautiful. And she was, too.

DAMON AND VANDALIA

Damon

They came out of the darkness past the bamboo patch so like a fistful of spears, and as they threaded a path between Clark's battered yellow Volkswagen and my blue Peugeot, I saw she was carrying a plastic bag filled with some sort of grain—rice, perhaps. Clark rose to meet them; wind swooped from the incline and blew the kerosene lamp out. I stood up, a reflex I didn't know I had—old world charm surging in this colonial, barrel chest—and stumbled over the ice bucket. Drunker than I realized. Bourbon and Texan heat go devilishly well together, a gentle pair passing practically unnoticed, leaving one languid and curious.

But all this unexpected activity. I stumbled, fell to one knee; in the warm, vegetal dark I stayed, palms pressed tight around the sweating aluminum bucket until they ached from the cold. What seemed to take centuries: a male drawl, then her voice, upbeat, saying *birdseed*; Clark's laugh *I must give both of you a hug come here*. Then I was on my feet again and walking towards them, unsummoned, hands dripping and a chest spiked with gasps. It was a scene to be repeated in endless variations— she await, earth's bounty in her arms; I bowed, my hands cupping all I had to offer—gifts that changed their form even as I held them out to her, stones melting to tears.

Vandalia

That evening of high wind and heat, I was finely tuned to every sound, every movement, merry and skittish as a school

30

girl without knowing why. My mood pleased Michael, and he smoothed his neat afro and tried on his new smile, the one that went so well with his professor's pipe. The bamboo stood guard, a pale green organ in shadows.

We drank a lot. Somewhere around midnight, Clark ran out of ice and the trays lay forgotten on the back steps, condensation spreading in an ever darkening stain. The creek sang its ghost song, calling for a sign from the sky. Lukewarm whiskey, now, in tall glasses. The wind gushed, diving into the chimney of the lamp. We took turns lighting the wick; my fingers shook as I slid the wooden match from its box. Damon began to chatter in Japanese—I thought he was talking gibberish, until Clark said he had spent his childhood in Japan—and then I found him pretentious. Without saying so. And each matchstick a long-stemmed, unopened rose.

Damon
Protons and electrons—barometers of the human body, scientifically proven aphrodisiacs and depressants: the heavy, dragged-out feeling before a summer storm—and afterwards, the air discharging and you with it, purpling ions, all is electricity. More and more often she came from the city, escaping the proton-laden skyscrapers and traffic, her hair crinkling from sweat, her brown skin as glossy, each day a bit darker, as the bark of a cherry tree. By the time she reached our place the negatively-spiced air of the countryside had taken effect, and she showed no sign of exhaustion or tension. It was as if she were high. She told me that she was frightened of cacti—the flat peppery lobes, the tufted spikes—and that she found the drive through the mesquite wasteland strangely exciting, like the exhilaration of a soldier after surviving a battle.

Vandalia
Michael, his pipe and his southern inferiority complex. Talk right, learn to play tennis, never lose control. Make something of yourself. There's a way to "go about" everything.

We were to meet after his faculty meeting and I had chosen the bar. I should have known The Diamond Cowboy could only be what it was, booths of black leather and men in tight jeans dancing with each other, their tooled boots shuffling across the dark red floor. I ordered a Carta Blanca and sat down to wait. Then Clark came up. He danced expertly, Mr. Cool, just like a black dude. He was cruising and I was waiting for

Michael; we bolstered each other, ignoring the others so as to appear more desirable.

Then Michael had come, and I could tell Clark liked him and that Michael was jealous. I didn't explain, not at first. Clark bought a round; Michael began to loosen. *You'll have to come visit me,* Clark laughed, his arms around both of us, *in my love nest in the country. And meet my boyfriend, naturally.*

Damon

I was born in Japan of a father who loved all that wasn't England and a mother doomed to follow him, but determined to take England with her wherever she went. We travelled throughout the Far East in service of the Company. It was a childhood of seas and pine woods and mountains, of inscrutable manners before all adults and spankings when I slipped out to play with the Japanese children. Those children bullied me mercilessly. I was Gulliver among the Lilliputians; they expected danger in my robust British frame and so they struck before I could or would, or so they thought. (But I was tame—oh, I was tame and stupid with my rosy cheeks.) I loved them so, those children, and I wanted to be like them—small and dirty and full of abandon and laughing as they pinched and kicked me. In the English school, haven for diplomats' sons, I excelled in running and in debate; alone, in bed, watched by the chill pine, I spoke Japanese like a sailor, cursing fiercely into the crisp pillow.

Vandalia

Our neighborhood was a garden of smells—the rank smoke of the rubber factories, the grapey breeze that passed for spring, the witch-water bitterness of collard greens—all these thick scents mingled and clung to the skin in silent collusion.

And in the endless alternating shifts in the tire factory, six to two to ten to six, I was born—a change of pace, a breath of fresh air in the lives of my parents. And in the accepted custom of lower-class black families, they chose for their daughter a name that would stand out, a name suited for the special fate awaiting this child, their contribution to history, and so they named me Vandalia. Vandalia the vivacious, the valiant, the vibrant. A lightness and a treachery, like the beguiling flames of a snowstorm. Softly: Vandalia.

Until fourth grade geography, when a classmate went up to the map to point out Chicago and instead cried out *Look, here's*

Vandalia!, and everyone wondered, and the teacher took me up to the map so I could see for myself. Later, in the public library, I looked it up in the encyclopedia: A city in south central Illinois, seventy-five miles southwest of Springfield, on the Kaskaskia River. Dairy and grain region. Founded 1809, enjoying the position as state capital 1819-39, now the seat of Fayette county. Industry: cereal production and the manufacture of transformers, shoe heels, clothing and telephone booths. Population 5,160 (1960 census).

I thought you knew, the teacher said, and what I felt was shame. My parents and their neighbors had never ventured beyond the once-thriving canal town of their youth—one had only to look at my name to see. And I had thought I was unique, a fine joke. At least 5,160 people knew how ignorant we were.

Damon

When I was old enough I was sent—as a punishment, it seemed at the time—"home." Education in Eton. The neat quadrangles, the livid lawns boxed in by stone, grey and raw. At last to be dwarfed, to look up to Something. The autumn evenings, the deep and aching blue through the dormitory windows, booze and philosophy in small spaces, the sharp animal scent of wool and male bodies warming the room, their sweat as stimulating, as exciting as a strong black tea. My roommate moaned in his sleep; I dared not rise and comfort him.

Later I fled across the Atlantic to central Canada and its furred creatures, lakes to fish and woods to fell, enough wilderness to get lost in—for three years, when it spit me out and over the border to North Dakota, where I thought I'd die until I learned to turn my fear to good use and began to run—to train until the heart-muscle swoll to meet the fear, beating to the *tropp* of track shoes on cinder, *endure, endure*. Marathon runner. Time to think of nothing but the body's thunder.

I ran my way to the university; I knew I couldn't escape it all along. Track scholarship—and again the slap on the ass and the innocent guffaw, the slick knotted thighs and the gang showers and the hair in the eyes, stinging, and the smell of strong black tea, that cool lightning at the base of my spine. I trained. I ran until my chest threatened to burst; but when I finally collapsed into knees and elbows on the grass next to the high jump pit, he was waiting, smiling, with his boy's face and his long slim legs.

33

Vandalia

My job—the job that buys my freedom from the industrial midwest, from factory smoke and acrid stink of simmering greens—is to type filmscripts into a computer. Green letters, squarish stencils poured through with light, appear on the darkened screen. When the screen's full, I read it for mistakes, type them over—and the computer inserts the corrections, the lines readjusting automatically to accommodate the addition. I type the entire script on an ever-rolling scroll of light impressions, and when it is finished I print it out—the laser printer spitting out a page every few seconds, perfectly typed pages of eight-and-a-half by eleven bond with the appropriate margins and numerated and italics where indicated, the whole shebang.

A job unrelieved by physical contact or mental strain, a job of our time. I devise ways of coping; I pretend I am a sculptor, gaze into a block of blackish green marble until my gaze meets resistance, and so defining contour. I type in obscenities, I invent dialogues between the barber and his philandering wife and erase them the moment before Print Out. Though increasingly I have to admit that I feel nothing while I am typing; it is no more probing the stone as it is writing in air.

Damon

I change jobs like drinking water—and wherever I go, what the tap brings forth tastes different—smooth with fluorine, salty from the pump, sweet as the brook running through pine woods (or is it the brook that runs through childhood, the rush that comes when one is unfamiliar with the world, a not-yet-tiredness), the metal-sour smack of reservoir fluids pulled from pits on the outskirts of town and strained from one steel tank to another, the liquid flowing clearer and more anonymous with every filter.... And as I grow accustomed to the new flavor of a drink I regard as delicious, yes, vital, something fades, life balks. So I break camp; I shed skins.

The jobs I've had: waiter, lumberjack, student, gardener. Whenever I needed money I did free-lance translations—instruction booklets for Japanese imports, from cassette recorders to automobiles through to the inevitable cameras.

But since Clark, I've languished under a curious lassitude, content to let whatever happens happen, the demands of the moment sluicing over me like a sexual flush. When Clark got hired as a curator at the University of Texas, I followed him to Austin. I followed him to the garden house in the country and took the hammer he held out; I planted the herb garden *parsley sage rosemary and thyme*. I accepted the duties assigned me, cook and mechanic and romantic foreigner.

Vandalia

Clark knew. And said nothing, silently accepting the gifts I brought, shamefaced tribute. It was a habit I had learned from Michael's friends, liberal white intellectuals who went to Europe each summer and brought back quaint rules of etiquette: they could never accept a dinner invitation without showing up with a box of chocolates under their arm or flower heads bobbing, distressed, over a horn of blazing tissue paper.

My gifts were unusual—a reflection, says Michael, of my trusting personality. Now I outdid myself. Seed for the bird feeder. An olive retriever, metal jaws on a long stem. A wicker jar for crickets. Crayons, forty-eight in a yellow flip-top box.

Damon did nothing, all day. Hung around. Whenever I came, my latest ornament carefully presented for Clark's carefully registered delight, he was lounging on the back terrace. Walked in casually, hands balled in the deep pockets of his khaki pants, shirtsleeves rolled loosely below the elbows and the collar open, revealing a reddened vee of skin and the first crisp curls of chest hair. How strange that a man who tanned so easily should burn right there. And he never took his shirt off.

Clark knew without asking what I wanted, running around the kitchen in his ill-fitting jogging shorts, chopping limes, sloshing tonic over a tower of ice cubes. A half hour, no more. Else Michael would worry something had happened to me on the road.

And everytime he appeared in the back door, fists in pocket, I knew he had been waiting.

Damon

Clark is gone. He came back from the supermarket with a bag full of fruit, among them limes, a netted sackful. Said he couldn't stand it anymore, took a sharp knife and slit the throat of the net so the limes spilled all over. I scrambled for the rolling limes and Clark stood there, watching as I gathered them to my lap, a palette of fragrant green. Then he turned. *Get it over with*, he said, walking out.

35

Vandalia

A cold fish, my mother frowned, following the flattened pear of a white woman's buttocks down the street. *Couldn't warm up an ice cube, much less a man.*

It was the morning after Labor Day and we went downtown to shop for last-minute school supplies—and maybe a dress for me, if any decent ones were on sale. I was ten and she thought I didn't understand. I didn't—but I remembered until I was old enough.

She said it in self-defense, unaware she was rubbing a little brighter the myth. I think she was even proud, who knows...this woman who wanted so much to learn that she taught herself French with the help of a tattered primer found at a rummage sale, calling out the names as she laid the groceries on the table: *oeufs, jambon, pommes de terre, poulet.* No word for turnip greens. No word for chitterlings, for sweet potato pie. A woman with so much and nowhere to give it but her house and family, what she'd been taught was enough. And I her daughter, cold.

Damon

The third day. Again Clark did not come home after work; for two days he hadn't returned before ten or even midnight. No words had passed between us; we were both exhausted. The knife lay next to the bowl of limes, exactly where I had placed it.

All day the sky had weighed on the earth like a large sweating hand. And suddenly, without warning, water loosened over the house—a wonder that flattened the weeds and released a cool, metallic perfume. The roar was deafening. From sheer nervousness I ran outdoors, peeling off my shirt and throwing it into the herb garden. Bare-chested I was monstrous, a Caliban; I held back my face for the rain to pelt eyelids and cheeks, throat and forehead. I was a harpooned whale; I wanted to be drummed blind.

Vandalia

The cloudburst overcame me as I turned into the driveway; I switched off the engine but kept the ignition on, watching the windshield wipers plough a dry space that was promptly inundated again. All a matter of timing—if I blinked, counterpoint, to the blades' click, the windshield was always clear. I sat for five minutes or so, blinking. On the seat beside me stood a birdcage constructed entirely from toothpicks, each sliver individually stained and varnished. There was a ladder inside the cage, leaning against one side, and a tiny wooden swing. The swing moved in time with the wipers....

The yellow Volkswagen was nowhere to be seen but the Peugeot was there, blue hood well into the bamboo patch. Had they gone away for the weekend? I could walk up to the door and check. Or I could drive back. In this rain.

Damon

All I remember is that I took the birdcage from her and set it on the table. I was dripping, shivering; I asked her if I could get her something, a towel or a drink. Then, of course, it was over too quickly—she moved slightly and I overran her; I nearly swallowed those gasping lips in my efforts to find the contours inside the skin. She drew back instinctively, her mouth and chin slick and glistening from my kiss and I apologized; *forgive me* I said again and again, as I licked from her neck and ears the salt and bitter of sweat and cologne. For an instant I thought of those cold and wet Japanese winters spent whispering into the crook of a pillow; I had never been more terrified.

Vandalia

The thundering around us and the silence between. He stood in the door to the terrace, bare-chested, the red vee of collar skin an arrow pointing down, down, and his khakis soaked and wrinkled, clinging to his legs. It was as if I were there and not there at the same time; I watched and felt myself being watched, I closed my eyes to disappear.

When we had finished, he placed his palm between my legs, cupping and defining, his face as wondering as a child's, amazed that that's all there was—no magic, no straining muscular desire.

It is possible we have never met. It is possible that this is fiction and, though we are always moving towards each other, the scene will fade at the last moment. There are times when I have not left the car, when the birdcage of sticks does not swing, buffeted by the rain, when I have not entered the house with Clark gone and the limes waiting on the counter, exhaling their insidious perfume.

Damon

When I am with Clark there is consolation—the same bones beneath the same skin, how they float around, or rest quiet, or tense.

Now I know I am not modest though I pretend to be. Now I know I did not follow Clark to Texas but led him there; we ran away together but I pointed out the way; I chose the spiked and prickling desert as our retreat, I pressed for a house in the countryside, I glimpsed the wild bamboo, luxuriant, beside the creek and said *This is mine.*

I could not make a move until Clark spilled the limes over the kitchen counter, but then I moved. Now Vandalia is the one who waits—and when it doesn't happen, the thing she was waiting for (but I'm not sure even she knows what it is), she begins to grow vague, her eyes looking only at the surface of the world, not the world itself, not me, and I've lost her, again.

What I think about when we make love: the blip fading on the screen. What I feel: Vandalia flattening, spreading into a map, the map of my longing. Her skin is taut as a mask and mine is loose over its bones like an elephant's. The small of my back curves into her until there is nothing left. And I am small, small when she touches me.

Vandalia

It is summer; I have done something wrong. *Wait till your father gets home* my mother says, and sends me to my room. Instead, I wait for her to disappear down the basement to check on the laundry—then I slip through the door and down the front walk. Quiet. Asphalt softening in the sun, undulating like black greased waves. A tar smell.

Across the street is a vacant lot with a maple tree in it, the flat starred leaves casting an irregular circle of shade. I go to this tree and climb it; I swear never to come down again.

For a while nothing happens. The broad leaves are cool on my arms and legs. The tar smell mixes with the non-smell of air. What does it mean, to do something wrong? I am alive but I am never where I think I am—for instance, I am not in this tree, I am far away. The six o'clock whistle blows and father's Buick comes trundling down the street; now things will happen.

The screen door slams; *Vandalia* they call. I will not come down I am not here. Where I am the streets are swept and flowers line the windows. There is a Sears & Roebuck where

I am, and a soda fountain and in the center of town a grassy square with a white bandstand right in the middle, and around the bandstand green benches but no one is ever sitting on them. I walk down the glittering sidewalk and everybody knows my name. *Vandalia*, they say, again and again.

THE VIBRAPHONE

Christie Phillips was a student in musicology—concentration baroque. Her parents never knew what to make of this—to them, gospel was the only serious music, and whenever she went home to Toledo, they would try to drag her to their AME church to play the organ.

The requirement in college to master at least three instruments had led Christie to the harpsicord—and suddenly she was plunged into the narrow yet measureless world of early music, where embellishment rippled into formata, where time changed to suit one's mood.

When Jerry Murdon had his debut at Carnegie Hall, Christie managed to get a ticket, even though the concert was sold out. Murdon had all the promise of young genuis—piano study with the best teachers at Berkeley and then Juilliard, first prize at the National Bach Competition for young performers, several years' experience as a soloist at Spoleto. Half of the female music students at the prominent music schools in the country were in love with him. "There is nothing," the critics were fond of saying, "to keep Murdon from becoming one of the greatest pianists of our time."

At Carnegie Hall he burst onstage, correct and handsome in tails, his reddish afro like an explosion under the spotlight, a tensed authority in the jagged face. He seated himself, long curved fingers poised for the Bach Sonata in D Major... there was silence. Silence that deepened and chilled the longer he played, for there was something different in this familiar music when he played it—something pepped up, askew. Stunned silence, then, and finally, hissing. Husbands walked out; their wives, some actually in tears, followed more slowly. Jerry Murdon kept on playing; the concert was being recorded and the sound engineers let the tapes run, more from a morbid curiosity than any sense of duty.

Columbia refused to release the tapes; they bought themselves out of the contract, and Murdon used the money to produce his own record. He called his label Lunar Discs—a reference to the fact that Bach had milked his eyes blind copying music by moonlight. The album jacket showed Jerry Murdon at the piano, tails flying and afro exploding, in the far-right corner of a starthick sky a hovering full moon, and the man in the moon was Johann Sebastian Bach. The title spilled across the sky in cobalt script: "Recreation of the Soul. Murdon Plays Bach."

Of course Christie bought the album. The record became a hit. It was Bach of the twentieth century—industrialized, anonymous, defiant, the playing technically exquisite. She tried to duplicate certain passages on the conservatory pianos but always came away discouraged. When, on his next LP, Jerry Murdon switched to electric piano, she switched with him.

Five years Jerry Murdon dominated the jazz scene, his Bach interpretations growing more estranged. Then, quite suddenly, there were no more concerts, no more recordings. His rivals claimed he had run out of ideas; gossip columnists predicted yet another victim to drugs. *Billboard* magazine reported seeing him on a beach somewhere in Italy. No confirmations nor contradictions were made in this chaos of wild speculations; Murdon, wherever he was, kept silent and the public, disappointed and just a bit insulted, dropped him. Jerry Murdon, King of Bach, was soon one of the forgotten.

In the meantime Christie had started on the theoretical section of her dissertation, an analysis of her own transfiguration of an obscure seventeenth-century Italian instrumental "opera" for harpsichord, viola da gamba and baroque flute. The composer was very obscure indeed; most of the documents weren't available. She grew tired, discouraged, and humiliated; more from despair than the hope of finding any material, she finally applied for a summer scholarship to conduct research at the musical institute in Florence...and was accepted.

Florence was like walking through an oil painting, one of those thronging street scenes radiating with color and the newly-discovered landscape of perspectives. She had more than enough time to decipher those manuscripts waiting for her; September was two weeks gone and the days still warm...what better time to take off for a weekend?

That Friday she took a train to Pisa, made the obligatory snapshots of the tower, then caught a local bus to Viareggio. Viareggio was like any Italian resort town—a beach littered with beer cans, tar and seaweed and—parallel to the beach— the promenade, a broad avenue lined on either side with expensive jewelry stores and bright boutiques.

It was too windy for swimming; the beach was deserted. She turned back towards town. Immediately behind the promenade, the city sprouted into a thicket of smaller, grimier streets where the Italians lived and shopped. She wandered around, looking for an intimate cafe, something—when, about two blocks away, a black man with a dog stepped out into the street—his long head, the reddish afro, the silhouette so familiar from a distance....

He was gone. She quickened her pace; but the street she thought he must have turned into was empty. Perplexed, she returned to the corner and walked slowly to the spot where he had appeared. She was standing in front of a music store.

The small round man behind the counter looked at her with a patient, dubious smile. "L' americano?" he repeated, scratching his head.

"Si," she said. "He's a pianist, isn't he?"

"Paese," he replied. He took her to the door and pointed up the street energetically.

Several times she stopped to ask an old woman or a passing school child the way to Paese, for the street had a maddening habit of dissolving into spidery alleys. Finally the last stucco house was behind her and the streets curved upwards sharply, into the vineyards. There she stopped and put out her thumb.

A cherry red Alfa Romeo pulled over and a middle-aged man in a slinky shirt rolled down the window: "I'll take you wherever you want, signorina!" No other car stopped for a good fifteen minutes. Then she got lucky.

A battered, three-wheel pick-up halted, and a young man in baggy white overalls and paint-splattered boots opened the door. He was employed at the new villa going up outside the village of Paese, where he hauled plaster every day and once— about this time of day, three or four—the Black American with the dog....

The pavement was broken in places, and for a while they rode in silence, the pick-up slamming hard into the rutted path. Directly outside the village, they stopped.

"This is as far as I go, signorina."

"But—the American?" she stammered.

"This is as far as I took him, signorina. As far as Paese." He hesitated. "The signorina has been looking for the American for a long time?" His voice grew dark, solicitous.

"Not really. That is—"

The disappointment in his face surprised her—what had he been expecting? Then it hit her: in his head an elaborate melodrama, a scenario in the operatic mode, was brewing. She gasped and swallowed at the same time, bringing tears to her eyes.

"Signorina!"

He held out a hand, checked himself. She buried her face in her hands.

"Signorina, don't cry! Please."

A hand on her arm, patting it as a child pats a doll.

"Don't cry," he repeated, his voice hardening. He put the pick-up in gear. "Don't worry, signorina. We will find him."

Pulling up in front of a crumbling pink church at the village square, he got out and walked over to the neighboring cafe where a group of old men were playing dominoes. The consultation was brief; he returned smiling. The path led through Paese and out the other side, where the road became a dirt trail twisting still higher into the mountains. After another ten minutes of hairpin curves and teeth-jarring potholes, they pulled up behind a rusty Fiat parked at a delapidated gate that seemed to hang in mid-air, suspended by a wilderness of overgrown vegetation.

There was no bell, no mailbox. The gate stood ajar, and beyond it she could just make out the flagstones of a walkway curving through the trees. Christie stepped through the gate. The air was heady with the mixed scents of rosemary and rotting olives. The path swerved to the left.

A bright, clipped lawn, as neat as a starched tablecloth. Rows of flowers, perfectly ordinary daisies and petunias. Dainty white picket fences encasing the plump beds and even a rose arbor.

The house was less spinsterish, two stories high, stone whitewashed to blinding perfection. It was abnormally long and its length was punctuated, from roof to foundation and from pole to pole, with windows.

Then it came, out of nowhere. Music. Sounds wrung from joy

and light and squeezed through voltage meters, a whine that twitched like electrocution and sobbed like a maniac; music that robbed the air it rode upon, vibrations that rattled her breath and shoved it back down her throat. It was a sound that made the garden, in its innocent stupidity, glow like a reprimand—a warning from a lost childhood or a lost love, or anything as long as it was lost, lost....

"If it bothers you, I can turn it off."

He looked older than forty—he had grown a beard, which was black, and the reddish afro, his trademark, straggled dully around the mistreated cowl of a speckled gray sweater. The beginnings of a paunch. Hips sunken in, lips full and somehow vulgar in the haggard brown face, dimples cutting along the sides of his cheeks like scars.

He went back inside. A moment later, the terror had stopped.

He reappeared. Wordless, he led her into the house.

The music, and the sight of him so suddenly near, so changed, had acted as an anesthetic. She didn't know what to think of the situation, though curiosity and the thrill of adventure helped placate the small anxieties trying to surface.

They entered a large room, airy and bright, an ideal studio. But it was full of reel to reel tape recorders and electronic devices—dubbing machines, splicing decks, amplifiers. Wa-wa pedals littered the floor like poisoned field mice, electrical cords squirming in a maze towards every corner.

Jerry Murdon moved through the room flicking switches, plugging in cords, adjusting tone levels, checking balances. He came to rest at a vibraphone in the center of the room.

"The motif," he said, picking up the mallets. She recognized it as the organ prelude to the fifty-second Cantata: *Falsche Welt, dir trau' ich nicht.*

"—And here it is again."

He flipped a switch and the melodic line, amplified, wailed from massive quadrophonic speakers. He flipped another switch and the same melody, shaken and broken down nearly beyond recognition, rose from the floor. Another switch, another— and a roar of sound, grace notes proliferating like bacteria, chords like a dying train, poured over her...and beneath it all the characteristic undulation of the vibraphone, its relentless throb taking over her pulse.

"There they are, twenty-four from one. A single source. Can you find the core again?"

"I've—I've lost it."

44

"But it's there. It's there, you can tell, can't you? Don't try to listen; feel for it."

She nodded, weakly. He went over to the back wall and pulled a lever. The music stopped.

"See that hatch?" He pointed to a small square in the ceiling directly above her. "That's where it all goes. Come on."

He led her upstairs. At first she couldn't make out anything; the shutters were drawn. Then she saw a bed, unmade, and an aluminum ladder hanging from hooks on the wall. She jumped—something growled. Red eyes glittered from the pillow.

"Quiet, Sebastian!"

The dog grew still. He walked over to the bed, knelt beside it and threw open the trapdoor. The light from the studio streamed up.

"At night," he said, softly, "I open the hatch and let my latest composition come up. Then I fall asleep and dream the variations." He smiled, his face suddenly very young.

Christie looked at the blazing hole; it seemed to spread towards her. "Don't you ever"—she searched for the right word—"get seasick?"

He laughed. "The throbbing, you mean? That's the beauty of it. To float on the lap of the sea, to move with the pitch and reel. To stand up in the center of things with no point of gravity but your own." He slammed the hatch shut.

"Would you like some tea?"

This room was much smaller. There was just enough space for a table—a hexagonal, carved mahogany piece of oriental design, and two tall leather chairs whose curved backs and armrests were covered with intricate tooling.

"Have a seat—be back in a sec."

She sat down; in the center of the table stood a shallow dish filled with black candy drops. Licorice. She counted the pieces.

There were exactly twenty-four.

Christie looked around, suddenly uneasy. The windows were covered. Panels of heavy dark red cloth were draped from floor to ceiling to create an illusion of a six-sided space, like the table. Brocade dragons scaled the cloth panels.

Jerry Murdon returned, tea things aloft.

"It's not so often I get visitors; I must take advantage of you."

"In what way?" she asked, lightly. She looked over the tray he had placed between them—smoked oysters skewered with toothpicks, black olives, sesame rounds, cheese cubes. A bottle of something clear and alcoholic. Cigarettes.

The tea pot exhaled an acrid perfume, Jasmine.

"You see," he said, pouring the tea, "I realize you didn't come all the way up here for nothing. Perhaps you came because you're a bored, spoiled little American who thought it would be a blast to see how old Murdon has degenerated...."

"I'm a music student," she said, lamely.

"So," he replied, leaning back, "a music student. Piano, I suppose."

"Harpsichord. I play in a baroque consort."

"More than one way to get at the core," he said, nodding. "Bach, of course, was the purest of them all—but baroque was better than what came afterwards. That maniac Beethoven obscured vision for over a century. Would you like some vodka?"

"No, thank you."

He poured himself a drink. "So why don't you tell me what brings you here."

"I'm studying in Florence." Christie hesitated. "It wasn't easy to find you."

"I can imagine," he countered. "Therefore I won't let you get away unrewarded."

She reached for an oyster, not daring to look him in the eye. He waited, enjoying her discomfort. She thought of her dissertation, in a box in her room in Florence. She thought of the pale sandwiches at the Trattoria. She thought of her first violin, she thought of the first Murdon album with Bach as the man in the moon...but none of these thoughts stayed in her mind long enough to count as a full idea. He lifted his shot glass and tossed it off.

"Don't worry," he said, relenting. "You came for my story, didn't you—why I left, how I got here, the whole deal, right?"

She nodded.

"Now then—you might remember, being a fan of mine—" he threw a glance at her, testing—"my keyboard style changed three times during my career. First, of course, there was the classical perfection of Jerry Murdon, the best young pianist of a generation. Then the furor at Carnegie Hall, my real debut in more ways than one. You see, I knew what I wanted; I was just looking for the right break. Colleagues called me an opportunist, critics called me a confidence man. Remember this article?"

He opened one of the table's drawers and extracted a newspaper clipping. "'First he encourages our outrage by his circus antics at Carnegie Hall; now, assured of our attention, he has set out systematically to destroy all that Bach has created. Where, I ask you, in this cacaphony, this parodic bebop, is the spirit of that great man who said he composed "for the glory of God and the recreation of the soul?" What Jerry Murdon is doing amounts to blasphemy.'" He put the clipping away. "Fools," he muttered.

"My second change was in many ways more dramatic than the first. It came a year later, a scant three months after my smashing success at Newport." His dark eyes fixed her like a specimen moth. "My playing became—how shall I describe it?—less agitated, more melodic. One *Downbeat* critic dubbed it 'The Golden Age of Murdon.' The real story begins here. It begins with a woman, naturally.

"She had heard me at Carnegie Hall and was convinced I was a genius. She was tall, attractive, Italian-Jewish descent. She did textile prints for the big ones—Cardin and Blass. Her faith in me was exciting; indeed, her complete trust spurred me on in more than the musical sphere. I began to see other women, although Elizabeth satisfied me completely. It was an irresistible chain of events; her very submissiveness lured me into more affairs. I was unscrupulous; I wanted her to find out. But she never noticed anything—an intelligent woman, mind you—she chose never to notice anything. I would come home at seven in the morning, stinking of martinis and perfume, with some tale about a new piece I had been working up with the band, and she accepted my story—even if the drummer had phoned the night before to ask where I was.

"I shocked no one except, perhaps, myself. No reproaches, and the thrill fades. Betrayal became time-consuming and, eventually, boring...so I stopped. Enter the Golden Age."

He lit a cigarette. "Contrary to the rumors circulated by the press," he added, wryly, "I have never been very highly-sexed."

He pulled the smoke deep into his lungs, leaning back to let it drift down his throat before pushing it out again in a thin gray stream. "When I am making music, I have no time, no room, for anything else. My body disappears. You could call it a by-product of creation. I'm sure, in fact, that if someone investigated the matter, they would find out that God, the supreme artist, has no penis." He smiled. "What is creation after all but a godly act? And what do I need with the pitiful palpitations of human tissues and fluids when my music"—he sprang forward in his seat—"when my music will last forever?"

He leaned back, that youthful look on his face again. Innocent. A fawn.

"Cases of sexual disinterest are not so uncommon among artists. Dylan Thomas, for example, neglected his wife—and every other female of the two-legged species—whenever he was engrossed in a poem. And when he had finally written the last line, drunk and freezing in his drafty shack in the Welsh countryside, the rush of creation still glowing, that incredible deranged energy tingling in his groin—do you think he remembered Caitlin, fair and lonely in their farmhouse up the hill? Do you think he thought of a warm bed and the soft words of love?" He paused for effect. "No—he masturbated."

Determined not to give him the satisfaction of showing her shock, Christie held her face impassive. He turned aside abruptly and grimaced. She sipped her tea carefully.

"I finally had what every man or woman of genius needs—a wife."

"So you married her?" she asked, naively. The triumphant look he shot her made her wish she had kept her mouth shut.

"I don't mean marriage contracts and golden rings. I mean wife in all its philosophical implications—that circumstance in which another soul serves as a standard, a foil by which to measure one's progress—or, if you will, one's aberration. I mean the home one turns one's back on, the slippers one kicks aside. The person who believes in you unconditionally. In colloquial terms, a wife."

He paused. "Those were the *cantabile* years. Four years—a perfect quartet. The highest praise"—and he reached in the drawer again, spreading the clippings on the table, articles from *Jazz Monthly*, *Billboard*, *Village Voice*, *Downbeat*—"was written then. When things were almost over. Oh, there were signs. I was dissatisfied. My last record was listless, secondhand, and I knew it. The third stage flared up—a return to the *prestissimo* of my post-Carnegie days—but my technique had more style than...well, brilliance or profundity. I was afraid.

"Then without warning, a woman dies. Elizabeth finds a letter in her mailbox from the attorney in charge of the woman's estate. I didn't think she knew anyone west of the Alleghenies, but there it was, black on white—a sixty-five year old woman dead of asthma complications in Phoenix, Arizona. Elizabeth was an heiress—no considerable fortune but an interesting one nevertheless—namely to all the household and personal possessions of one Mrs. Aaron R. Rosenblatt."

"Her mother?"

He snorted. "Elizabeth was alone in the world. Her parents had died long ago. More tea?"

She shook her head. "I'm ready to try the vodka, please."

"Wise decision."

The room was very still. Was it soundproof?

"When I asked her, Elizabeth claimed she had been just an acquaintance, an old neighbor from Brooklyn for whom she bought groceries when she could no longer get around. 'O.K.' I thought, 'I'll go along with that.' It was my turn to believe unconditionally.

"We flew to Arizona. Elizabeth wanted to go alone, but I argued that there were certain business details—liquidating the condominium, for example, or deciding the fate of a six-month old diesel Mercedes—where two heads would be better than one. Besides, I had just finished my fifth record, 'Murdon's Requiem' and I needed a break. 'A little cactus juice will do me good,' I joked. Reluctantly, she agreed.

"I had never been to the Southwest before. It made a very powerful impression on me—a barbarous landscape, raw and beautiful as a baboon's ass."

He looked up, his eyes fierce, bloodshot. "Our great civilization, with its skyscrapers and automobiles"—he was smiling now—"seemed no more than a huge, complicated toy. Mrs. Rosenblatt's condominium complex looked like a battery of cereal boxes hastily set up to ward off a hurricane. We located the correct building, obtained the keys from the manager and let ourselves in. It was an apartment like any other—prefab walls, balcony, built-in shelves, dishwasher and freezer. Color T.V., glass coffee table. At first glance there was little we saw we could use ourselves—maybe the music box from Austria, shaped like a breadbox, with interchangeable melody rolls. Elizabeth discovered a camera with the film still in it....

"We moved on to the kitchen. Spotless formica, stainless steel sinks gleaming like sunken mirrors. A woman who kept things up, who would never be caught off guard by unexpected visitors. The kitchen yielded a few odds and ends—a very good old-fashioned meat grinder, like the one my grandmother used, a waffle iron which baked scalloped cakes imprinted with interlocking hearts.

"On to the bedroom, then. A dressing table with the usual assortment of talcs and perfumes, a jewelry box with a ring in it, a diamond in an overladen setting. In the closet, tucked behind polyester pantsuits and cotton sundresses, a very nice mink coat. Elizabeth didn't even want to try it on. 'What's wrong?' I asked, teasing. 'Don't tell me you're superstitious.' 'I don't like mink,' she snapped, walking out of the room. I had never known her to lose her temper before.

"But I was patient. You see"—he fixed Christie with his bloodshot eyes again—"it was my turn to play wife.

"I decided to explore the rest of the apartment. The bathroom was typical, pink tiles and the smell of bath salts and disinfectant. At the end of the hall a broom closet—nothing to see there—and next to it, opposite the bathroom, another room. The door was shut but the key stood in the lock, so I turned it and pushed the door open.

"The shades were drawn. A single bed, made up like an army cot, stood to the left, the blue blanket folded in a precision envelope and laid at the foot of the mattress. Next to the bed stood a night table, but no lamp. Likewise a bureau against the far wall, devoid of ornaments—no lamp, no knickknacks, no doilies. The very barrenness of the room, couched in the half light of a day turned dingy by window shades, made me realize how full of life this 'apartment like any other' had been so far. 'Strange,' I thought, 'a guest would hardly feel comfortable here'—and that's when I saw it, in a niche in the far right wall....'"

His voice trailed off and his gaze, directed towards her but not seeing, was the gaze of the poodle on the bed, a reflected and opaque brilliance.

"The niche," he continued, softly, reverently, "was hidden by a heavy black cloth, with a fluorescent light fastened to the wall above it." His gaze focused briefly, slid away again.

"I went over and lifted the cloth. As with everything Mrs. Rosenblatt owned this, too, was in perfect condition; but there was a difference—for, although the keys' high sheen testified that they had been wiped every day, though the felt damper bar was free of dust, the mallets had not been placed in their holder but lay ready, both pairs, across the keys. As if someone had just left off playing. All this I saw and registered automatically; only much later, in my New York studio, did I put together the entire constellation.

"I found the cord and plugged it in. The discs in the pipes slowly began to turn. I released the damper pedal so that the keys could resonate, picked up the mallets, arranged them to strike perfect fourths. First a C scale—the fourths were nice, and I liked the curious lurching tone of the vibraphone. I was just about to try a few chords when I heard Elizabeth scream in the living room....

"There was a freezing stillness, then the sound of running steps in the hall. She stopped at the door and hung there, holding on to the sides of the doorjamb with both hands. Haunted, face drained of color, she stared at me. Then she fainted.

"By the time she came to, I had carried her into the living room and begun to administer all the first aid one learns from the movies—a cold towel on the forehead, cognac at the lips. She came to and smiled. When she remembered she jumped up, hysterical, and demanded to leave the house. I complied. What else was there to do? We got into the car and drove out of the condominium village, into the desert. The endless vistas of scrubgrass, the wild, magic mountains, seemed to soothe her. I, too, was calm, but it was a calmness of despair. I had lost something—I was certain of it—but I couldn't put my finger on what. We drove for nearly an hour. I think we drove in circles; the same adobe ruin loomed up at rhythmic intervals, a caved-in hut with a spot of bright green—a scrap of cloth or a candy wrapper—wedged between two bricks. I said nothing; there was nothing for me to say.

"They had met at a jazz club—one of the countless smoky cellars in Manhattan where young musicians go to try out their wings. He played with a group that did commercial jazz; he was much better than the others. She went up to him afterwards and told him so. They talked. His name was Daniel Rosenblatt."

Christie shifted her position; the chair was very hard. Misreading her restlessness, Jerry Murdon sniffed and laughed shortly.

"I know. It sounds like the typical love affair. In a way, it was. They moved in together after a few months. He took her to meet his mother, who was upset until she learned that Elizabeth was technically Jewish. Then the mother began to hint marriage. She hinted for seven years. Seven years! Finally, they decided to get the license—but first, they said, we'll take the honeymoon. When we come back, we'll tell her....

"Where can a young couple go after seven years of blissful shacking up? Somewhere sunny, somewhere south—but not the Bahamas, not Capri, no—a place with a difference. That's when Elizabeth remembered the other half of her blood—

peasant blood, her father's, and her grandmother's tales of a life in the mountains, surviving from olives and wine. That's how they decided on Italy."

Tuscany, Christie thought. Paese. *Here.*

"Well, they left Mama in her mink on the airport observation deck, wringing her hands, and to Italy they went—on the beach in the morning, on the mountain paths in the afternoon, and at night in restaurants, wining and dining themselves silly—saltimbocca and fritto misto and canneloni, capuccino in the morning and expresso at night.

"One evening, Daniel decided to have a pear for dessert. There was no reason for either of them to suspect anything; the restaurant, listed with the tourist office, even boasted two stars. The service was swift and polite, the meal impeccable. Who would have suspected that the fruit had been washed too hastily that evening? Who would have thought a simple unwashed pear could breed on its blushing surface such a rare bacillus? Back in their room, Daniel complained of pains in his stomach. An hour later, he couldn't move his legs...."

Murdon lit another cigarette, flung the snuffed match on the floor. "She telephoned an ambulance and rushed him to the hospital. His stomach had stopped hurting; but he was numb up to his nipples. The doctors were helpless. 'A virus,' they said, throwing up their hands. 'Where can we start, there are a million of them in the air...' By morning, Daniel Rosenblatt was dead."

Christie watched the cigarette disintegrate, unnoticed, between Murdon's fingers. Was he lying—was the entire story merely invented, a noble allegory of his jumbled ambitions and private doubts? For all the pathos of the story there was also a coldness to it, something structured—as if he had gone over it many times, revising and ornamenting, lying on his bed in the dark with the amplified swell of twenty-four vibraphones frothing below him.

"Now that she had told me," Murdon resumed, the words issuing from his lips almost mechanically, "she felt better, almost cheerful. The energy with which she took charge was baffling. She contacted the lawyer and turned over the management of the remaining personal effects. She decided to keep the Mercedes. As for the vibraphone—Elizabeth's suggestion was to take it to New York with us, where it would bring a better price. I was put in charge of selling it.

"Back in Manhattan, it was as if nothing had happened. She never mentioned Daniel Rosenblatt again, and I never asked.

I put an ad in the *Times*, set up the vibraphone in my studio, and waited. But every time I opened the door and saw a prospective buyer's anxious, hopeful face, it was Elizabeth's face I saw, terrified and inscrutable—and I wouldn't sell. When I remembered that face I couldn't practise, either. Instead I sat and looked at the vibraphone, its thirty-six steel plates, those churning columns of sound. What I couldn't understand was why she had never talked about him before. We were an enlightened couple. There was no reason, no reason at all.

"After two weeks had passed, Elizabeth asked me if I had had any luck. I said I had someone coming in in the morning who seemed interested. The next morning I withdrew 3,000 bucks from the bank, gave her the money and told her the customer was satisfied. Then I went to a bar in Soho and got drunk. That night I slept in the studio."

Christie's head was pounding, a dull, wrenching pain to match the thump of her heart, a muffled yelp—but it wasn't her heart at all. It was the poodle, barking at the other end of the hall.

"Quiet, Sebastian!" Murdon yelled.

His hand trembled as he reached for the vodka bottle and his voice had an edge to it. "I taught myself to play vibraphone," he said. "I had to play; it was the only way out. I stayed in the studio. When I felt hungry, I heated up a can of soup; when exhaustion overwhelmed me I fell asleep as I was, the mallets in my hands.

"I was asleep when she knocked. I remember it was late afternoon, because the sun slanting through the windows struck the instrument and threw bars of light and shadow on the floor. She demanded an explanation. She began to cry. She said I had to sell it. She begged me to stop playing. 'I can't stop,' I said. I was telling the truth, but she didn't believe me."

Murdon reached for a drawer. A vicious tug sent packets of letters, bound with red string, spilling onto the rug.

"They're all the same," he said, pushing the letters together. "Variations on a theme. She can't leave me alone; but she can't come to me, either. So she writes to me. My fan mail," he whispered, gazing at the heap of envelopes.

He stood up abruptly. "If you'll excuse me, I have work to do."

He was kicking her out; shocked, disappointed, Christie picked up her purse and followed him downstairs. He opened the door and stood back to let her by, his face a contemptuous mask.

"They all go in the end, with their tails tucked under," he said. "Don't flatter yourself. You're not the first one to seek Murdon out in the wilds of Tuscany. Every summer someone shows up, sits still and listens."

Christie held out her hand to say goodbye but he stood transfixed, leaning against the door and staring at some point beyond the arbor. "It's the strangest thing," he whispered. "I talk and talk, and you listen. But you never tell anyone else, not a peep"—his face twisted suddenly—"his spell is that strong."

The door closed. Christie turned and began walking slowly down the path. Behind her, the music started up again, that surging, choking wail, a clamor against wasted innocence— she shivered looking over the garden—a search for the contentment lost long ago, without anyone knowing it.

ZABRIAH

Zabriah shows up at the Euclid Arcade, dry though the rain is pouring outside; she waits for someone to notice her and some do, shying away from a woman who looks like a man, a black woman with lint in her nappy hair and one shoe in her hand, a woman built like a pissoir, squat and round and something to be vaguely ashamed of. It's supposed to be summer isn't it, ISN'T IT! she screams, not sure she's spoken at all; no shout reverberates in the muffled roar of the arcade under itself, in the rain, Saturday shoppers going about their purchasing, the vaulted esplanade like the inside of a submarine, the shops ranging in tiers of iron filigree and illumination blooming in the rosettes of art nouveau lampposts; there is room here for every corner of the globe, Brazilian briefcases and Californian soy bean bread, German harmonicas and Swedish napkin rings.

Where Zabriah moves the walls bulge to receive her, the floor rumbles, the air makes room; but what good does it do to circle and circle in ever higher tiers, where does it get you? Zabriah is not tempted by stair case tracery or the membrane, sky-colored, ballooning overhead; she knows where she is going, let someone stop her if they can, all the way down, clack of a heel and thump of a sock, to the other end of the arcade.

They're up to something in there, through that window—hands folded, eyes turned inward, the towering books and a woman in a pale suit at the end of the table, her mouth nibbling at the words printed—Zabriah can't quite see them but she knows they are there—on the papers in her hands. One has to be careful here, one wrong move and you'll find yourself laid out on a marble slab, cold; she opens the door a crack though and what she hears is poison *Black milk* the suited lady is saying *of death we drink you* careful now slip inside *drink you evenings we drink you and drink you* Zabriah bursts upon them, drops her sack of a purse on the floor, holds tight to her shoe though: Is this the Poetry Circle? Yes, they answer, all the pink rabbit eyes blinking, yes we meet every other week, volunteering information, telling this creature anything as long as she leaves them alone; Zabriah feels sorry for them but she has to do this, slamming her shoe on the table. Well I paid my annual dues last December and never heard nothing from you people who's in charge here?

Matt stands up slowly, inclines his head kindly to one side; his name is Matt because a button on his shirt says so and another, directly below it, pleads LOVE A JEW TODAY and Matt stands there for awhile, smiling. He is seventy-five years old and poet since his retirement from the post office; he knows every book published in the English language on Fascism and the Holocaust and it is Matt who says We have no leader but you're welcome to stay and listen.

Zabriah sits down, breasts and beads spilling, she folds her arms, pushing up the sleeves of her sweater, the woman in the suit repeats *Black milk of death we* and Zabriah interrupts, Ain't nobody Black around here.

This is a poem, the lady explains. By a German poet, Paul Celan.

Don't remember him, Zabriah says, shaking her head. Is he one of those concentration camp daddies?

No! He was a victim of a concentration camp, and the black milk in this poem symbolizes—

Ain't no Black fang coming down these days, Zabriah mutters, picking up her purse. You speak German?

Yes, I do, the lady replies.

I know German, too, I know German and Russian and I've seen the Warsaw ghetto. Do you want to hear my jew song?

Later. Matt polite, intervening. First Mrs. Moore, then Mrs. Carmichael—

—And if you *really* can speak German, Zabriah continues, eyes boring into the silk bow arranged above the suit as one arm, elbow-deep, digs into the belly of the purse until it finds what it was looking for—then, of course, you know calligraphy.

A pause. What—you speak German and don't know calligraphy?

With a heave she pulls out a handful of matchbooks, lines them up all in a row, counts them, scoops them into her arms and stands up. Don't say a word, don't giggle she's coming this way and she's hurting pretty badly, is she lame or is that just the shoe, how she lists to the right, going like a mudslide, don't swallow don't jerk, how young she is, nineteen, maybe twenty....

Everyone gets a pack of matches but they aren't allowed to touch them until she leaves, slamming the door as she goes. The room exhales, the lady finishes *your golden hair Margarete your ashen hair Sulamith* and it's Mrs. Carmichael's turn, in a high quaver reciting *I chanced to see a butterfly/Asleep upon the sill*; everyone is bored but what can they do, Mrs. Carmichael is a regular, she comes every time, twice a month, armed with a sheaf of poems written in royal blue ink. *To think that beauty comes so small* she exclaims as Zabriah slips in again, listening patiently for three quatrains before pronouncing: Classical bullshit. And: Love for everyone. And: Let me tell you this ain't the buggy age no more this ain't even the auto-industrial age, this is the jet age. Spaceship twothousand-one, put five million on it. Bitch. Got it? Helicopters.

Zabriah strikes a match, lets it drop onto the royal blue poems and Mrs. Carmichael's eyes go wet. Matt jumps to put it out: Who do you think you are, Zabriah asks, the reincarnation of Moses? but Matt doesn't care, he's clapping his hands for attention and stomping his feet and calling out Now it's your turn turn it loose sister! and Zabriah throws off her shawl; she throws back her head and for an instant is beautiful as an ocean liner is beautiful, ablaze and sinking:

> Wa-too-wa-too Lee
> Ho Chi Minh—Ha!

grinding an obscene jelly roll as she punches her fists again and again into the air, making room:

> Deep in the Cherokee valley
> Don't you know my name is Jimmy

she's been to the Warsaw ghetto, she's been to calligraphy school, your ashen hair Sulamith, she sings the same words over and over. Matt starts up a collection, holding out a glass ashtray, come on everyone give a dime a quarter a nickel, Matt himself puts in a dollar bill, sets the tray before Zabriah as she sinks into her seat Sister what a marvellous voice that is, it reminds me of the great gospel singers, Mahalia Jackson...

After all that exertion she's not even breathing hard. Who? she asks, quietly.

Mahalia Jackson, he insists, you remember her....

With a sweep of the arm that sends coins and ashtray spinning Zabriah stands up, fixes Matt with a look he's beginning to understand.

I don't remember anyone over the age of twelve, she retorts, pivotting on her one good heel and marching, sallying forth under the voluminous skeleton of the arcade, its airy parabolas, its invisible drums, its iron angels sighing.

AUNT CARRIE

The train! The train station with its iron and glass! Still invisible but roaring it came, and the roar grew louder. It roared, it rumbled, it growled like some wild thing. I thought it must be something much more terrible than anything I had ever experienced before. And as it roared out of the dark direction of Pittsburgh I knew that I had always thought of Pittsburgh as something dark and roaring though I had never been there.

I was in my first train station. I couldn't understand why Aunt Carrie was there. Aunt Carrie, Mom said, had come along for the ride. What I understood even less was why Mom did not speak to Aunt Carrie. Aunt Carrie of the dark and wrinkled countenance. Aunt Carrie who no one believed was only six years older than my mother. Aunt Carrie: watery eyes, the smile with a missing tooth, the slight leer Mom said came from sticking her mouth where it didn't belong. She's always smelling her own upper lip, Mom said. I felt sorry for Aunt Carrie. She wore lots of lipstick to make herself look pretty but she wasn't, her face sagged.

How come Aunt Carrie hadn't recognized my drawing? My father had a moustache ever since I could remember. It was thin and curved, like two rat-tails. Maybe my lines were a little shaky and his mouth was a little crooked, but it was him, no mistake about it, and I had drawn it from memory.

"Your father doesn't have a moustache," she said. Of course he had! What kind of aunt was she?

A garbled announcement came over the loudspeaker. The

train was rolling into the station. And that train carried my daddy.

"It's time to go," said Mom in a weird voice.

We descended to the platform. There the cool stale air swept upwards like the breath of the underworld. Funny that it was cool.

Aunt Carrie had taken out a hanky and was twisting it—that looked funny. We waited on the platform for the train to come and stop. And it came and stopped and it was not like the long and awful sound that had come before it. It was like the movies when the light shines cheerily from its one eye and the squeal of the brakes is exciting, and the people pour off and into other people's arms.

I fell into my father's arms. "What did you bring me, what did you bring me?" I screamed, because he himself seemed too terribly still, too far from me to kiss. I needed some souvenir, some proof that he had actually come from Pittsburgh. He'd brought me his name tag. "Ernest Price, Goodrich" it said. His shoulder smelled of pipe smoke whiskey cologne and hair pomade and very faintly, the train.

"Your lovely sister's here, too," Mom said, and I thought she sounded even stranger than before, her back arched in the last stages of pregnancy, her belly pushed out tight against her white blouse. Aunt Carrie stood a little to the side, her coat still buttoned. I could barely see her.

"I happened to read an interesting letter she wrote you a while ago, Ernest," Mom kept on saying in the strange voice. "I thought it only proper that she come, too."

Daddy tightened and then pushed me away, gently, but it was still a push. They were going to have an argument again, except this time it looked like Daddy was going to cry, and I couldn't stand that. No one moved. They stood still so long I got fidgety and wanted to run, but I didn't know who to run to, they all looked so strange. Aunt Carrie was pulling on that hankie for all it was worth and then I could see that she was crying. It wasn't nice for Mom to call her lovely when she wasn't. That must be what they're going to argue about. I had a pain in my stomach. I wanted to go home.

* * *

"What do you take in your tea, Aunt Carrie?"

"The same as you, dear. I don't take much to tea usually—never had occasion to, I guess."

"Would you like something else then?"

"No, thank you, dear." She chuckled. "You must have learned this in the Big World."

"Learned what?"

"Having tea in the middle of the day."

"Listen, Aunt Carrie, I want to apologize for not getting in touch with you sooner, I mean, right when I got into town. I've been so busy—"

"Don't go apologizing to me. I'm not one for apologies, makes me blush. You young people got all that life ahead of you, it's no wonder you're busy. We know how it is. We may talk a lot about you not coming to see us and all, but we know how it is." She took a handkerchief from her purse—small and white with a pink rose in one corner. She dabbed at her eyelids. "I remember when I used to babysit you you liked to draw a lot. You drew up every piece of paper you could get your hands on. Your Dad had to lock his desk."

I watched her hands. They wrapped one corner of the hankie around the right index finger, pulled it straight, started again with the left index.

"I meant to ask you a question, Aunt Carrie," I said.

"What, dear?"

"Why my parents moved to Florida when I was nine, right before my little sister was born. I never figured it out, really."

"Your father got an offer—"

"I know that story." I watched her hands. Sometimes the rose could be seen among the twisted ends of the cotton, a delicate blemish. "But I also remember a summer day in Ft. Myers when I was playing in the flower bed under the kitchen window. I wasn't supposed to be there, which is why I didn't stand up at first when I heard my parents' voices inside. They were arguing. Dad yelled that he had settled for less and had left his home town just because of her, and now she still couldn't—and then he walked over to shut the window and saw me kneeling there. He didn't say anything, just stared. Then he shut the window. They didn't talk much for months."

I poured myself another cup of tea. "I thought over that scene often, but I never dared to ask anyone about it. Neither him nor, heaven help me, Mom. Do you know what was going on? You were with us at the train station when it all started...."

Aunt Carrie stopped twisting her hanky abruptly. She became so still that I knew I was very close to the secret—if I only persisted. I looked into Aunt Carrie's eyes.

"I need your help," I said quietly.

The stilled figure in the corner of the sofa became a little more erect, and a sigh, barely audible, issued from her lips and hung like dry scent in the air.

"It's hard," she whispered. She straightened her back a little more, placed her hands in her lap and like a schoolgirl reciting her lesson began to speak, her voice trembly at first but gaining strength:

"I thought about it a lot. Not when it happened. When it happened, I didn't think about nothing at all. No one did. But afterwards, I thought about it. If you remembered the night at the train station. If you could make sense out of it at all. If your mother ever mentioned me to you. It was so hard not to be able to talk to anyone about it. It happened so long ago. I didn't mean your mother any harm. I couldn't have." She took a deep breath. "I thought a lot about how I would tell my side if anyone asked. I knew I couldn't cry or get indignant. It's nobody's fault. Long ago I decided that if anyone asked me, I would tell everything as I felt and saw it from the beginning.

"My daddy—your grandfather—ran off at the beginning of the Depression. I was thirteen, your father was nine. Mama began taking in washing, cleaning up white folks' houses—anything to bring in a few dollars. My older brothers and sisters were married off or sent to find work as soon as they were old enough to walk without wetting their pants it seemed. I had seven brothers and sisters older than me and I never saw them much, except on holidays. Mama let me stay home and take care of Ernie—your Dad. He was the smart one in the family and we all loved him the best. Ernie was our shining star, and we did everything to protect him from things. So I stayed home and took care of him while Mama went to work. I cooked him breakfast and sent him out to school, and tried to help him with his homework. Ernie never heard a harsh word about his Daddy—in those days men left their women for all sorts of reasons...and nobody blamed them much, because times were hard. But when Ernie finally learned that Daddy had left us holding the bills and the babies, he went furious and never spoke his name again.

"I was the runt of the family and the homeliest. I knew it—no one had to tell me. I could see it in the mirror and in the eyes of people when they came to visit. So when your father got to be grown enough to fix his own breakfast, there was the problem of Carrie. What can she do? Not smart enough for business, not pretty enough for marriage. But they found me someone to marry, finally. A widower, forty-two years old, who ran a barber shop. Numbers racket on the side. I was seventeen.

"Folks said Sam Rogers was a good soul. He'd lost his wife of twenty years to an accident and was helpless without her. He needed a woman to clean and cook and to give him a little comfort in the declining years of his life. I was perfect, folks said. In a way, moving into his little house was so much like living at home that I barely had to adjust. He come home at night and I'd have a good dinner waiting for him—Dixie butter peas from the garden and baked yams, chitterlings on weekends. I washed his clothes and kept the house clean. He barely noticed me. It was like taking care of my baby brother.

"Everyone thought I was coping so well. The older ladies would wink and ask me how I liked having a man in the house, and I'd smile. I didn't let on that Sam hadn't touched me. Not that I minded. Sam Rogers was big and sweaty, and when he sat down at the dinner table I sometimes thought of a big slimy frog. He had bugged-out eyes that were bloodshot—not from drink but because the air and dust could get to them so easy—and he grunted when he walked, almost like sounds would help him along. But he was kind, and I got used to him. Little by little he began to come out of his grieving. After a few months he began talking about his wife's cooking. 'Could you fry me some green tomatoes for tomorrow?' he'd ask. 'Edna used to make them.' I asked around to find out how to fry green tomatoes, and they'd be on his plate next morning. 'You cook nearly as good as Edna,' he'd say, and it pleased me to know I was doing a good job.

"Then one summer evening after dinner he was sitting in his chair and I was on the sofa, crocheting a doily for the armrest, when he turned to me and said, 'I want to tell you about Edna.' I put down my handwork, and he was hunched down in that chair so that his head nearly touched his knees, almost as if he was in pain. He talked about Edna when he first saw her, at fifteen, and their wedding, and the baby that died because she hadn't know what to do and couldn't get into town to a midwife. He talked about how she lost all her shyness when the lights were out. I sat there and listened to him, a great big piece of a man humped over in that chair like a child with a stomach ache, talking about what ailed him. He must have talked for hours. It began to get dark. Do you know how twilight makes the air look like it's full of feathers? Everything seems to come apart and float around, and heavy things like tables and chairs take on a grainy look, like old sugar. I listened and watched Sam melt too, just like the furniture. He seemed so delicate all of a sudden.

"When he finished he looked at me without sitting up—just turned his head and looked at me from his knees. He smiled. Then he laughed. Then he reached out his hand and I went to him.

"I got to tell you all this because you've got to see what it was like. I mean, I'd been taught for so long to be thankful for whatever I got that I didn't think to ask for more out of life. I took whatever came to me and was satisfied. I didn't know what I was missing. Which was why, a couple years later, I about went crazy when he up and died. Lord knows I didn't have the world, but the little piece of it I had I didn't want to give up and have to start all over again. But there I was—a teenage widow with little money.

"So I went back home. I kept house and helped Mama with her washing sometimes, and I babysat the children in the neighborhood. Everyone started calling me Aunt Carrie. Aunt Carrie was there to do whatever needed to be done. Ernie was fifteen by then and was growing in his sleep it seemed like. He was near to six feet already—and handsome, slim and tough with straight black eyebrows and broad shoulders. But he was too serious for his own good. Every spare moment his head was in a book. He studied so much that it got so he looked a little cramped, like some twisted-up fungus that grows in the dark. He looked pale under his color—ashy. For all his book learning, though, he didn't know beans. Never went out with girls...never even looked at them. People'd say, 'That boy's going to make something out of himself,' but I'd worry."

She paused, and for a moment the sound of laughter came from outside. Boys in the street, their feet slapping the pavement, small thudding sounds clustered together, a shout....

"Anyway," Aunt Carrie continued, "spring came—not spring exactly, just the first blowsy days. I'd been washing sheets and had hung them out on the clothesline. But like I said, the weather was unpredictable that time of year—clothes will dry in a couple hours if a rain don't come up and drench them, or if a storm don't appear out of nowhere and dash them all into the mud. That afternoon about three o'clock, it suddenly looked like it might rain. I ran outside and began taking down the sheets, when I happened to look up and see the most beautiful man in the world walking down the street. He had on a white shirt, and his head rose out of that white shirt like a statue. I felt myself go weak, and then I realized that I wasn't dead yet. I bent over the laundry basket, then peeked another look. He raised his free hand and waved.

"I was so confused and ashamed that for a moment I couldn't lift my head. I stayed bent over the basket, playing with the clothespins. I was ashamed, but the feeling wouldn't go away. I could have stayed right there, kneeling in the mud, and cried. But there was this feeling, this strength inside the weakness, which made me stand up and reach for the next sheet. Soon I sensed him next to me. He was playing around, joking—like he'd take down two pins at once and hold the sheet above the dirt with his hands and teeth. But then he reached around me to get my end of a sheet, and I felt the heat from his chest rising up against my back, and something went inside of me and I held onto that clothesline like I was drowning. He thought I was playing and tugged at the sheet. I wouldn't let go...if I had I would've fallen down. I stood there listening to the wind slap that sheet against my face, and I could feel the bottom of the sheet flicking my shins. It was like being caught in a sail, and flying, flying over everything. He gave up and let go, and I finally got it all folded and ready. He carried the basket inside for me. I must have walked funny, because he asked me if I felt well. I said I was a little dizzy and might lay down for a spell. He said he'd help me make the bed.

"So he took the basket into the bedroom and I went to the bathroom to try to pull myself together. But I didn't know what I was doing. I went in to splash water on my face and found myself undressing down to my slip. I could still feel that sheet beating against me, like a bird gone wild. When I walked into the bedroom, he was kneeling on the bed, trying to tuck the bottom sheet into the headboard. He whistled and plopped over on his back. 'I don't see how you women do this sort of stuff,' he said. I didn't answer. I was in a trance. 'There's nothing smells better than freshly washed sheets,' he said then, turning his head to the side and sniffing. He didn't suspect a thing. And without really expecting that I'd really go through with it, I bent over and touched his cheek. His face turned and looked into mine.

That was the first moment he knew anything. I remember seeing the pulse start up under his Adam's apple. And you know what he felt like to touch? Like onion skins. Soft and dry."

For a moment we sat without speaking. *What he felt like to touch,* I thought. *Soft and dry.*

Aunt Carrie's tone became brisker: "But that's what was important for me. What's important for you is what comes afterwards. We were together most of that spring and summer. I think he never really thought much about it. It was pleasant, and when it was over, he forgot about it. I'm sure of that. I stopped it because I realized it was crazy. I don't know if anyone suspected us. Mama was away so much of the time, and the neighbors thought Ernie was inside studying." She paused. "After a long while I got it out of my head, too, and when he married your mother there couldn't have been anyone happier than the two of them. When your mother asked me to babysit you and your brother, I didn't think about it at all. I don't know if I'm explaining it right. It was like it happened to somebody else—not to another me, but that he had been someone else."

My thoughts went in many different places. Was I shocked? But there were last questions—questions of routine, map-outs of procedure.

"How did my mother find out?"

"The time he went to Pittsburgh was the first time he'd been away from Belle since they were married. She was pregnant with your little sister, and she must have been lonely—I remember how clean the house was that week. When she got to shining up this picture of Mama, somehow she got it in her head to surprise him by getting a new gold-plated frame for it. That's when she found the note."

"Note?"

"To Ernie...a note I wrote him after the first time. Afterwards I was so confused, I ran out and didn't come back till right around dinnertime. When I got my senses back, I knew that whatever happened I had to make sure he didn't feel bad or that he'd been a failure...whatever goes on in a boy's head. So I wrote him a note telling how nice it had been—that he was a man now and should always hold up his head. I slipped it under his pillow. He must have thought about hiding it from Mama, so he put it where he was sure she wouldn't look— behind the frame of her own picture. It stood on his dresser for years and it went with him when he got married. I didn't know he had kept it. I don't know what he thought. But I know nobody would have known if it hadn't been for that note behind the picture frame." Aunt Carrie took a deep breath. "That night at the station your mother gave it back to me."

She sat very still in an attitude of waitful repose, her eyes straight ahead.

"I always wondered if you remembered that night." She spoke with her gaze focused on air, like a statue come to life. "Your mother couldn't be reasoned with. And your father loved her— he loved her more than anything in the world. He did everything to hold his family together—took the job in Florida, cut himself off from his kinfolk—I never saw him again."

I kept silent; I felt suddenly very relaxed.

"What did your mother have to say about me when you children were growing up in Florida? I know it's silly to care after all these years, but I'd like to know."

"She never said a word. We—" I had started to say *We forgot all about you.*

Carrie was nodding slowly. "That would have been the best way." A deep and irrevocable sadness. "Well, I'm your crazy old aunt." She paused. "Mrs. Evans always said you didn't know nothing."

"Grandma Evans?"

"Yes. She's the one who told me how her daughter found the note. She was there. When Belle called me up to ask if I wanted to go to the station, Mrs. Evans tried to stop her. 'Let lying dogs lie,' she told her, but Belle wouldn't listen."

Aunt Carrie laughed.

She laughed so hard tears rolled down her cheeks, and for a moment I was afraid she was going to be hysterical. Then she stopped, as suddenly as she had begun.

"I've been thinking about telling it all these years, and when it gets round to doing it I tell it all wrong." Her face turned to marble again. "After your mother handed me my own note back, she never spoke to me directly again. I didn't know how she had got hold of it, and I was too sick to ask. That night was the last time I saw Ernie, too, so I couldn't ask him. I don't know if I would've asked him if I could've. It didn't seem so important then. But later, after you all had moved and I had plenty of time to think back, I wondered. I didn't think I'd ever find out. Then your Granddaddy Evans died, and Mrs. Evans moved into Saferstein Towers. One day she called me on the phone. 'I'm lonely,' she said, 'why don't you come up for a visit?' I thought it was a little funny, but I went.

"She told me what she knew. She didn't want to hear my story. 'Old bones, dead and buried,' she said. So we became friends."

"Aunt Carrie—"

"Don't say nothing. I ain't expecting nothing."

I reached across the table, took her hand.

The old woman looked over at me slowly. "Honey—I have to be going."

This hand, soft and cold and dry. I squeezed it, gently. "I'd like to see you again, Aunt Carrie," I said. "I'll call you."

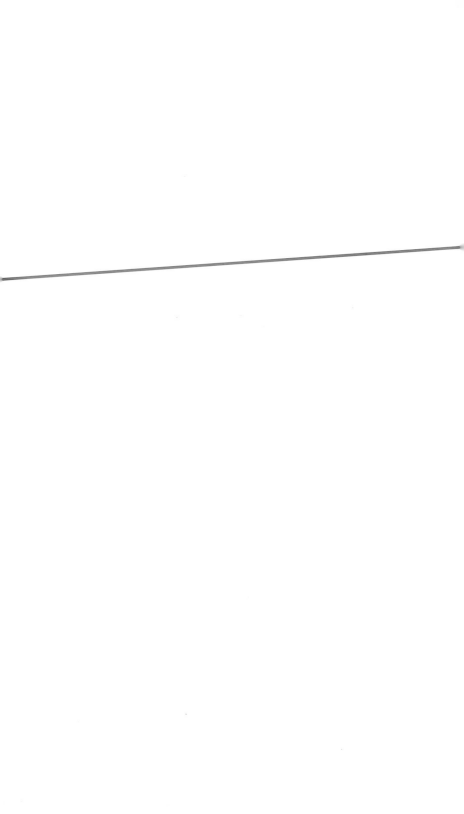

About the Author

RITA DOVE was born in Akron, Ohio in 1952 and was educated at Miami University (Oxford, Ohio), Universität Tübingen (West Germany), and the University of Iowa. She is the recipient of a Fulbright/Hays scholarship, and her poetry has earned her fellowships from the National Endowment for the Arts and the John Simon Guggenheim Memorial Foundation, as well as a Portia Pittman Fellowship as writer-in-residence at Tuskegee Institute. Presently she is a member of the editorial board of *National Forum* (the Phi Kappa Phi Journal) and serves as an advisory and contributing editor to *Callaloo*.

Ms. Dove lives with her husband and daughter in Tempe, Arizona, where she teaches creative writing at Arizona State University. *Fifth Sunday* is her first collection of short fiction.

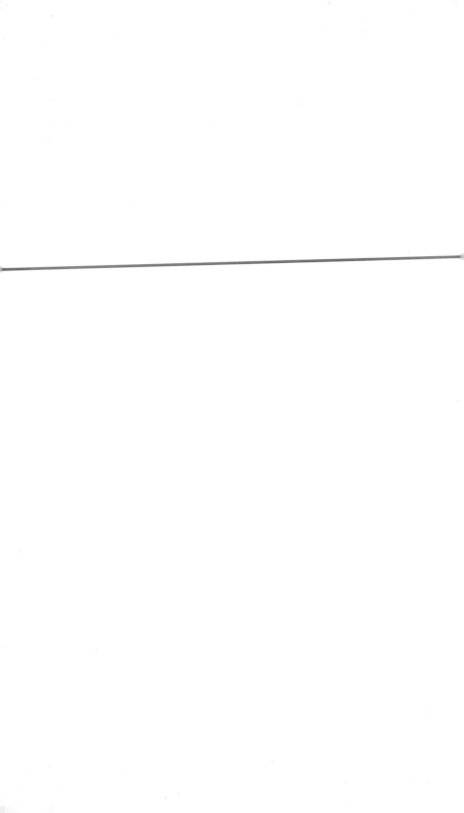